TEACHING SMARTER WITH THE BRAIN IN FOCUS

SARAH ARMSTRONG

■SCHOLASTIC

NEW YORK • TORONTO • LONDON • AUCKLAND • SYDNEY
MEXICO CITY • NEW DELHI • HONG KONG • BUENOS AIRES

ACKNOWLEDGMENTS

I would like to extend thanks to Laura Robb, who pushed me through the writer's gateway and encouraged me to put on paper the passion in my heart about teaching and learning;

Pat Wolfe for her generosity of spirit, knowledge, and ideas and for keeping her brainy bunch current on applications of brain-research in the classroom;

my editor, Sarah Longhi, for her guiding hand, insightful questions, and consistent support throughout the process;

my sister, Julia Reidhead, who coached me along the way and told me not to wait for the muse; but to just do it!

my colleague, Larry Barber, who read the draft and encouraged my efforts;

photographer, Meneta Deaton, and citation editor, Betsy Hrabe—friends indeed who helped me over numerous hurdles;

differentiation specialists and teachers in the Staunton City Schools who contributed to the book and from whom I learned so much;

my husband, Stu, family, and friends for believing in me and in this endeavor.

PHOTO AND ILLUSTRATION CREDITS

Page 6: © Visuals Unlimited/CORBIS; Page 7: © Nonstock/JUPITER IMAGES; Pages 11, 16 (top and bottom left), 17, 48, 69: © MedicalRF.com/JUPITER IMAGES; Page 14: © Index Stock Imagery/JUPITER IMAGES; Page 15, 54: © Meneta Deaton; Page 16 (bottom right): © Premium Stock/JUPITER IMAGES; Page 46: © Gianni Dagli Orti/CORBIS

Editor: Sarah Longhi
Copy Editor: David Kline

Cover design by Brian LaRossa
Interior design by Melinda Belter
ISBN-13 978-0-545-02120-3
ISBN-10 0-545-02120-0

2 3 4 5 6 7 8 9 10   40   15 14 13 12 11 10 09 08

Contents

Chapter 1

TEACHING SMARTER:
Moving From Good to Great Instruction

> If we succeed in leaving no children behind, it will be because teachers resolved to make it happen. The fact is, whether or not a child learns is determined at the closest point of delivery and that point of delivery is you—the classroom teacher!

IF OUR GOAL is to reach *all* learners, we must acknowledge that the way we have traditionally taught students has serious limitations. Research informs us that moving from rote to active strategies—hands-on learning, projects, discussion, higher-order thinking—has a positive effect on students *across* achievement and income levels, as well as cultural and ethnic backgrounds (Darling-Hammond, 1997). I am passionate about the need to give up trying to teach better, when teaching smarter is what's needed. I know as well that the thoughts I share have no substance unless you *buy in*. The good news is that many of you are eager to make this shift and are ready to forge ahead.

Walking this talk is essential to me, so when I consult, I coach teachers as both a model and a mentor teaching real lessons in real classrooms with real challenges. From kindergarten to high school—in art, science, English, and social studies—I develop lessons based on pacing guide and curriculum standards, teaching the class while the host teacher observes the recommended strategies with his or her *own* students. There are no prepackaged lessons and rarely is there a perfect class.

Years ago, I would have been nervous and reluctant to be a guest teacher in a classroom because of uncertainty about working with new students of different ages, the challenge of new content, and unfamiliar class dynamics. However, I've learned how to design lessons that focus on keeping students engaged and on task. After many years, I now have a repertoire of strategies to develop higher-level thinking and make *students* do the work of learning.

The result is that I started teaching *smarter*, not *better*—a distinction Linda Darling-Hammond, a researcher and consultant on teacher education reform, suggests in her work (1997). Her work recognizes that teachers expend tremendous time, energy, and resources in their classrooms, but emphasizes that schools will never transform if we simply continue to try harder, only to get better at doing what we've always done.

What is this "teaching smarter" all about? It's about replacing a traditional one-size-fits-all approach to teaching with a solid understanding about what helps develop students as learners. Teaching smarter is when you know how to take the strategic steps to consistently engage students and then designing the lesson to get the desired results. It starts with a mind-set, not a set of quick-fix techniques. Finding ways to do the same old approach better is not the answer this book provides. Teaching smarter steers us away from replicating the old slapstick comedy routine of answering the person who doesn't understand by repeating the phrase slower and louder. We cannot meet the needs of learners by teaching "slower and louder." Indeed, if we continue to rely on traditional methods of teaching, we won't make students more literate or better at math—and we'll certainly leave some children behind.

What Does Teaching Smarter Look Like?

Several years ago, I scheduled roundtable discussions about lesson design with K–8 teachers in four Virginia elementary schools and one middle school. I knew these teachers worked very hard and wanted the very best for their students, and I commended them for their efforts in trying to teach their students. But the challenges still remained: how to help all learners be successful, how to prevent student failure, and how to lessen teacher fatigue.

I told them that, to me, teaching was like peeling an onion—every time you think you understand what to do next, another layer seems to reveal itself and say, "Okay, now peel *me*!"

I suggested that these layers should be looked at as opportunities for growth and asked the teachers how much time they spent on planning from one day to the next. A new second-grade teacher teared up when she acknowledged that planning took an overwhelming amount of time. "I spend several hours a night just getting ready for tomorrow!" Many others had the same response. I then asked if they felt all these extra hours achieved the desired results. Some nodded unconvincingly; some shrugged as if to say "maybe, maybe not." So I asked the big question: "If you could spend the same amount of time—or maybe a little less—and get even better results, would you be interested?"

The teachers were intrigued, and our work began. Our sessions gave them tools to help them more effectively and efficiently plan lessons—and learning experiences for students—that would demonstrate *smarter* instruction. From my point of view, the part of our work that was most eye-opening for the participants focused on what instruction actually looks like when a teacher uses research on the learning brain to make decisions about teaching and lesson design. And *that* topic is the focus of this book.

Why Brain-Compatible Teaching?

Every once in a while we all experience that Aha! moment when all of a sudden something makes sense, or when in a lightning flash, the answer to a troubling problem is revealed. Realizing that research on the brain and learning has great implications for classroom teachers was this kind of experience for me—I *knew* from my first encounter with brain-based instruction that educators should be paying attention to research in the field of neuroscience.

It started nearly 25 years ago, when I heard a presenter describe the classroom of a right-brain teacher and the classroom of a left-brain teacher and how a right- or left-brain student might respond in each of these environments. She talked about specialized functions in the right and left hemispheres of the brain and I was hooked. I remember asking myself, "Could this right/left brain information explain why some students are more successful at school than others? Does it have a bearing on how students learn?"

After that, I tuned in to any discussion about brain-compatible teaching that I could find—many of which were presented in workshops about learning styles. Studies outlining attributes of right-brain learners and left-brain learners were published and some teachers used these lists to determine their own and their students' "brain style." I found the information interesting and novel—I didn't know how scientific it was, but I knew I had happened upon a kernel of truth and continued to pursue the topic.

My fascination with brain research led me to my dissertation topic on the brain and leadership styles, but my primary interest continued to be on the applications of brain research to learning. Questions persisted: *How do we learn? Why do we remember some things and not others? Why do some learners struggle so much?* At the time of my proposal defense, this "brain stuff" was not acknowledged in the higher education arena as having much merit, but my topic was accepted, and I started a more formal quest to learn what brain research could mean for educators.

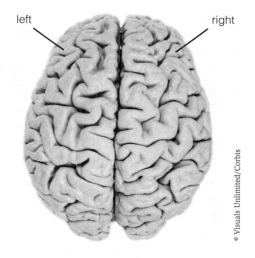

left   right

© Visuals Unlimited/Corbis

An early application of brain research in education was the contrast between "left-brain" learners (logical, analytical thinkers with a propensity for language, math, and science) and "right-brain learners" (creative, holistic thinkers oriented toward music and the arts)

Moving from stagecoach to sleek Ferrari could be a metaphor for what scientists knew 25 years ago compared with what is known today. In the 1980s, people involved in interpreting brain research for educators focused almost exclusively on the right-brain/left-brain distinction. At first, dialogue focused on the distinction between right-brain, global, artsy people and left-brain, linear, accountant types. It was suggested that teachers could determine if students were more right- or left-brained. Books on right-brain and left-brain thinking, drawing, singing, and moving encouraged teachers to teach to student brain "preferences." This initial round of books, though flawed, brought the brain-compatible teaching movement to "the street" long before most education bureaucracies would entertain a second look.

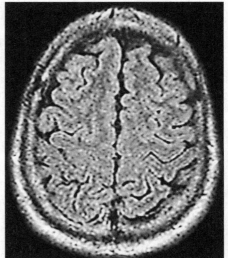

MRI scans highlight activity in specific areas of the brain.

Today, amazing technologies support non-invasive assessments of the brain in action. Through the use of PET (positron emission tomography) scans, which measure glucose utilization in the brain through radioactive dyes, and fMRI (functional magnetic resonance imaging), which secures images of changing activity in the brain, scientists can observe what happens in the brain during tasks of doing and thinking. For example, to answer the question, "Does the same sequence of firing neurons occur in the brains of dyslexic readers when they are decoding text as it does in the brains of healthy readers?" Shaywitz, using the fMRI, determined that the firing sequences for these two groups are distinct (2005). We have known that dyslexic readers respond to different instructional interventions than students who do not have the disorder, but now we have neurological evidence to support the need. This significant finding is one among many that makes a case for the differentiation of instruction for learners. The problem with one-size instruction is that it does not fit all brains!

A more recent technology, DTI (diffusion tensor imaging), reveals how the structures of the living brain communicate by monitoring the diffusion of water in the brain. DTI discerns the wiring of the brain and creates images of the connections among neurons (Valeo, 2007). The importance of DTI is that scientists can now track the sequence and pathways of how the brain talks to itself during specific tasks. Denis LeBihan, a leader in DTI development, states, "Right now we can see only the big highways in the brain, but we want to see every street" (Valeo, 2007).

Starting the Journey

Clearly, a key question from a quarter of a century ago still pertains today: "How can findings from research on the brain help guide teachers in the classroom?" Whether or not brain-compatible teaching should be applied is no longer the debate; how to do so most effectively is. My reason for writing this book is to prove that classroom teachers will in fact *teach smarter* if they design lessons focused on what we know about the learning brain.

When it comes to applications of brain research in the classroom, I think teachers are asked to absorb too much at once. Getting started is challenging, and a teacher who wants to move ahead with applying brain research may not know where and how to begin. I'm a big believer in the old adage, "Anyone can eat an elephant one bite at a time." Though I have no appetite for elephants, the adage illustrates that resolve and persistence pay off; efforts that seem enormous or insurmountable really aren't if you know which steps to take and when to take them.

The most important thing to know up front is that brain-compatible instruction will ultimately make your life in the classroom much easier and more rewarding. Following workshops I've conducted, teachers from all grade levels have shared their sense of "aha" when connections were made. A new middle school teacher came up to thank me and said, "I had this information in a class last year, but you made it make sense for me as a teacher." Another teacher shared, "Hearing the research on the brain and learning pulls it all together for me—*now* I know why certain teaching methods work." Similarly, in an evaluation response after one workshop, a teacher commented, "My assistant principal told me to use graphic organizers because it was one of the nine correlates to achievement from *Classroom Instruction That Works* [Marzano, Pickering, & Pollock, 2001]. I didn't know there was a reason based on how the brain learns. Now I get it." (We'll discuss the rationale for graphic organizers and other nonlinguistic tools in Chapters 4 and 6.) My hope is that every teacher will be able to say, "Now I get it," after reading this book.

More on Brain Research

Though this book does not provide a comprehensive overview of brain research and its application to teaching, you will find in the bibliography a number of publications on learning and the brain that provide excellent information on summaries of research studies that are relevant to educators, including up-to-date descriptions of brain-imaging technologies and results of recent studies on how the brain functions.

Getting to Brain-Compatible Instruction

The first goal of this book is to highlight significant applications of brain research to learning. The second goal is to provide guidance and examples of ways to integrate these understandings into daily lesson design. The questions that I hope to answer throughout the book are "What does this mean to me as a teacher?" and "How can I use it with my students?"

I would also like to pose four questions essential to implementing brain-compatible instruction in your classroom.

Are my students engaged in meaningful work? Meaningful work means that you design lessons so students recall and comprehend the content being taught. In the same vein, learners are meaningfully engaged when lessons are differentiated based on achievement and interest levels. What happens in the brain when students learn new information and are engaged in meaningful work will be discussed in Chapters 2 and 3. How to engage students through the activation of visual memory systems will be shared in Chapter 4.

Do I construct lessons so *students* do the thinking? Though teaching to the test seems all-consuming, building higher-level thinking into lessons on a daily basis is imperative. Strategies that encourage students to become creative and critical thinkers will be highlighted in Chapter 5.

Do I consistently make connections to students' daily lives? Helping students 'make connections to what they already know is a building block for new learning. Suggestions for activating prior knowledge are highlighted in Chapters 2 and 3. Although there is additional discussion about weaving these connections into daily lesson plans throughout the book, the importance of social interactions in making connections is discussed in detail in Chapter 6.

Do I teach so that failure is not an option? We must be tuned into the barriers to learning that students regularly confront, such as how feedback is provided and whether or not students have a clear understanding of what is expected. Our discussion about optimal brain-friendly approaches to help all students succeed begins with When Failure Is Not an Option (page 10) and is interspersed throughout the book.

I have outlined the lesson-design components on page 12 to help you begin to implement brain-compatible instruction in your classroom. These 12 reminders have the potential to make a remarkable difference in the lives of both teachers and students. These ideas are also presented as a lesson-design checklist in the appendix (page 124) and will be discussed in greater detail in future chapters.

When Failure Is Not an Option

Let's look at the fourth essential question, "Do I teach so that failure is not an option?" from the perspective of the brain and stress—because stress is a barrier to learning and persistent stress contributes to failure in school.

Picture a perfect classroom scenario: Everything is going like clockwork. You and your students are in sync and you have a sense of being in control. The lesson is going well, students are following the plan, and the classroom is calm, perhaps resonating with the steady hum of a well-oiled machine. Is this your reality most of the time?

Ask 20 teachers to rate their level of stress on any given day on a scale of 1 to 10, and I expect it is a rare occasion when even one teacher will take a Zen-like breath, smile, and declare, "Oh, I'm definitely in a low-stress zone—maybe 2." It just doesn't happen like that, does it? In fact, you and your students might experience any combination of the following stressors on any given day:

TEACHERS

- Missing a deadline

- Getting to the team meeting late

- Struggling with technology that isn't working

- Dealing with students who are picking on each other or acting out

- Worrying about the health of a loved one

STUDENTS

- Forgetting to bring in homework

- Missing the bus

- Leaving supplies in their locker

- Getting put down or picked on by peers

- Feeling tense when the teacher has to deal with an unruly student

- Not having a good night's sleep

Of course, this list of stressors could be much longer. The point here is not to dwell on the negative, but rather, to acknowledge that stress and anxiety are present in your classroom on a daily basis. Any time a student fails, negative feelings emerge that compound his or her stress level:

- I'm stupid.

- I don't care if I fail.

- Who needs to know this stuff anyway?

- The teacher is unfair.

- I had to take care of my younger sister last night so I couldn't do my homework.

- I don't understand.

And the list continues.

What does research on the brain tell us about stress and learning? When a person is under sustained stress, learning is impaired because the tiny, almond-shaped amygdala in the brain's limbic system cues it to focus on survival—basically telling the brain to hold off on any new learning because we're just trying to survive today! Dealing with an immediate crisis may bring out the *fight-or-flight* response—sometimes evident in a school or classroom when students instinctively respond to a perceived threat by punching or hitting. Chronic stress often results in excessive levels of stress hormones, such as cortisol, which can cause deterioration in key areas of factual memory (Sylwester, 2005). Prolonged stress can stunt the growth of dendrites, resulting in fewer connections from neuron to neuron and inhibiting learning.

The bottom line is, the brain's capacity to learn new information diminishes under stress. The goal then is to reflect on the degree and kinds of stress evident in the classroom and work on removing them as obstacles to learning. Be encouraged—teaching with the brain in mind can help strengthen your resolve to instruct students so failure is not an option.

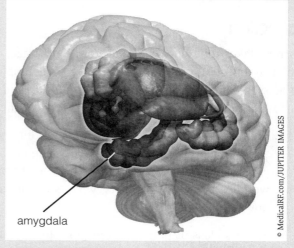

amygdala

© MedicalRF.com/JUPITER IMAGES

Registering stress, the amygdala cues the brain to focus on survival.

LESSON DESIGN COMPONENTS

✔ Know how students grow synapses when learning occurs.

✔ Understand the memory system and how students transfer new information into long-term memory.

✔ Recognize types of memory as a basis for using strategies to build recall of content.

✔ Activate prior knowledge.

✔ Use strategies which tap into emotions to improve memory.

✔ Use age as a guide for shifting the lesson focus to retain interest, encourage movement, and allow for processing of content.

✔ Use novelty to improve recall and engage students.

✔ Make the first and last parts of a lesson highly meaningful for students.

✔ Use nonverbal cues to enhance recall.

✔ Incorporate music and movement to enhance recall.

✔ Teach to the naturally social brains of learners to engage them.

✔ Understand that stress and failure in the classroom inhibit learning.

Reflection

Learning takes root when we reflect on, reorganize, or do something original with information. The reflection questions that follow each chapter are intended to help you internalize the message of each chapter through discussion and practice. Responding to these questions with a partner or in small groups will yield the greatest benefit.

1. Think of two or three areas of your teaching where you would like to shift from working harder to *smarter*. Think of one idea for each of these areas that will help you teach smarter. (For instance, you might be working harder at reteaching with workbooks and work sheets, when students might benefit from an entirely new or novel approach.)

2. Select a class or period and respond to these four essential questions.

   • Are my students engaged in meaningful work?

   • Do I construct lessons so students do the thinking?

   • Do I consistently make connections to students' daily lives?

   • Do I teach so that failure is not an option?

Chapter 2

ACTIVATING THE LEARNING BRAIN:
Using Memory Systems to Get to Mastery

WHEN I WAS in fifth grade my family moved to a farm in New York State, and for the first time in my life we owned horses. My mother was a skilled horsewoman, having learned to ride on a small Iowa farm as a toddler. My younger sister, Ginny, seemed to have the horseback-riding gene—particularly when it came to getting from the ground to the saddle. Ginny could put her left hand on the mane of the tallest horse and effortlessly pitch herself on top—in a split second, it seemed. Meanwhile, I would take my horse over to the front-walk steps, get on the second step, put my foot in the stirrup, and heave myself onto the saddle. My process was less dazzling and more procedural than Ginny's, but we both loved riding, and once in the saddle, both of us rode quite well.

My methodical approach to getting on the horse parallels the effort that most teachers must use to incorporate brain-compatible instruction in their classrooms. A few teachers have the split-second, almost magical experience of "Presto! I get it. I'll do it!" Many teachers, though, need to take the information over to the steps and climb aboard in a sensible, matter-of-fact manner. These steps will be part of our journey together.

Growing Synapses: Students Need to Know

How *does* the brain learn? Before I begin a lesson as a guest teacher, I almost always spend 15 minutes teaching about this very subject. Each time I do these introductions to the brain and learning, I am struck by how fascinated and attentive students are, regardless of their age or grade level.

A demonstration for upper-elementary students on how our brains learn typically goes like this:

- I explain to students that their fists represent the two sides of their brain—called hemispheres. The corpus callosum, which connects the two hemispheres, is approximately where the knuckles are touching.

- I ask students to put their left hand on the left side of their head. I explain that for most people, this side of the brain is the language center; expressive language (when we talk) and receptive language (when we listen) are functions associated with the brain's left hemisphere. "When you participate in a class discussion or you're listening to a lesson like you are right now," I tell them, "the language center of your brain is at work."

- I ask students to place one hand on the back of their head, just above the neck. I explain that this is the location of the part of the brain called the visual cortex, or the occipital lobe, which is activated when we look at pictures and view images. At times, I ask students to imagine the location of their favorite place to visit: "Close your eyes. Get a picture in your mind of the place you enjoy so much—perhaps the beach or a theme park." I inform them that even if our eyes are closed, as they are now, the visual cortex is still activated because we are recalling a picture from our past and there are specific neurons assigned to that image.

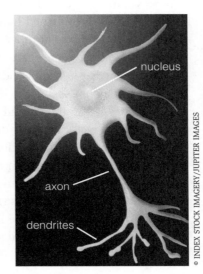

Illustration of a neuron

- Following my lead, students hold up their right hand with fingers outstretched to represent a neuron, or brain cell. The palm of the hand is the cell body, the fingers are dendrites (which receive information), and the forearm is the axon (which sends information). I then show students how a synapse is created in the brain by asking them to hold up their left hand. I tell them this hand is another neuron, and then I demonstrate how two neurons connect by touching the dendrites (fingers) of the left hand to the axon (the right forearm) of the other neuron and have them replicate the motions. As they do so, I explain that synapses are created when receptors on the dendrites connect to receptors on the axon—leaving just the tiniest gap. To finish the demonstration, I inform students that dendrites grow throughout our lives and that new synapses are created daily when we learn new things. "In fact," I add with a smile, "a teacher's job is to *help* you grow synapses!"

Students Remember!

In one class where I was guest teaching, a particular student was quite a challenge; he struggled to meet behavioral and academic expectations in all aspects of school. He was assigned a personal aide because he had difficulty focusing on what he was supposed to be doing, and when he wasn't focused, he distracted other students from learning. The teacher actually offered to have the assistant take the boy out of the class during my guest-teaching lesson to make it easier for me. I told her—lacking a touch of confidence, I might add, because I had never worked with the student—that I wanted to work in the same conditions she did. As I taught the scheduled social studies lesson, I asked this student to demonstrate a key point about the post–Civil War Reconstruction period. He dismantled a cabin of Lincoln Logs in front of the class to help illustrate that *destruction* comes before reconstruction. When he moved back to his seat following the demonstration, he seemed attentive. Following the class, the teacher said he was more engaged in my lesson than was typical.

Hand gestures show a synapse firing.

The story continues. A year later, I met this student—by then a fifth grader—at a new school I was visiting. He recognized me first and touched my sleeve as we passed each other on the steps. He said, "I know you. You are the brain lady. Do you remember . . . ?" and he opened his left hand and grasped his right forearm to re-create the model of a neuron making connections. While I was surprised at his recall, the encounter was another affirmation of my belief that students want to know—and will remember—information about their learning brains. Moreover, as they become more aware of how their brains work, they tend to take more ownership of their learning which, in turn, leads to improved achievement.

What Happens in the Brain When Learning Occurs?

One of our lesson-design components asserts that teachers should know what happens in the brain when learning occurs. The remarkable complexity of the brain suggests that any explanation about *how* the brain learns will be overly simplistic, but it is time to take what we know—limited though it may be—and use it to influence instruction in the classroom.

Let's elaborate on the explanation I give to students about how their brains learn. The brain contains 100 billion neurons that communicate with each other at junctures, called synapses. As you remember from the student demonstration, the synapse is where the receptors of one neuron connect with the axon of another to receive a message. Chemical signals occur at the synapse; neurotransmitters—including endorphin, dopamine, serotonin, and oxytocin—interact as messengers across the synaptic cleft, or gap. A single neuron has the potential to communicate across as many as 100,000 synapses (Ratey, 2001). However, some emerging dendrite branches and synapses are pruned or die off because of competition for the released chemical signals.

How do connections become more permanent? As neurons are exercised by the work of our brains, a fatty myelin sheath of glial cells (white matter) begins to coat the axon from the inside out and from the bottom to top (Sylwester, 2005). This myelination process is similar to the formation of rings in the trunk of a tree as it grows—the more a neuron is activated, the more layers of myelin rings surround the synaptic juncture. The result is faster, more efficient communication along the axon (Ratey, 2001). Thus, when students exercise their brains, fledgling connections become stronger—as the experts say, "Neurons that fire together, wire together!" Think of neurons firing as Web browsers making multiple hits on a single Web site. The stimulation of a synapse when a teacher reinforces content in many different ways can be considered instructional "hits." Just as Web site hits can bring a site to the top of a search engine, repeated rehearsal can make newly learned information more accessible the next time the learner needs it.

Neurons send information from dendrite to receptor via a synaptic cleft, or gap.

Our job as teachers is to help students grow synapses—by encouraging the development of new ones and making existing ones more permanent. This web of synaptic connections—which is continually reweaving itself—is influenced by genetics, environment, the sum of a learner's experiences to date, the content presented moment by moment in the classroom, and all other information bombarding the brain at any given time (Ratey, 2001).

Like the rings of a tree trunk, new layers of myelin form around the axon with each firing of the synapse.

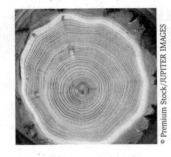

Understanding the Memory System

"I teach, but they just don't seem to remember anything" is a common lament I hear from classroom teachers. This is a big concern, because our job is to make sure that the content we're teaching ultimately moves into long-term memory. To be competent lesson designers, we need to understand the memory system and how students transfer content into long-term memory.

Alistair Smith (2005) describes the three parts of the brain that have controlling functions in memory:

> In retrieving memory, the amygdala, hippocampus, and frontal cortex are all involved. The amygdala assigns an experience an emotional "value." The hippocampus decides on where and how the information is stored. The cerebral cortex helps package the memory into a coherent whole. (p. 239)

Understanding the three terms, *value, storage,* and *coherence,* and their function is a key to helping students learn and fully memorize information. In order to commit facts and ideas to memory, students must value the information (is it interesting and useful?), have had enough encounters with it (reinforcement) to store it permanently, and be able to see the big picture to understand how all the pieces fit together.

The amygdala assigns value to information, the hippocampus stores information, and the frontal cortex packages the memory.

Let me illustrate with an observation I made several years ago of Becky Morehouse, a differentiation specialist, teaching a sixth-grade English class. Becky was instructing students about Bloom's Taxonomy, so that both the students and the classroom teacher could become familiar with the higher-order-thinking framework. The purpose of the lesson was to make sure students could identify and describe the six levels of the taxonomy.

Becky Morehouse's Hand Signals for Bloom's Taxonomy

KNOWLEDGE: Tap both temples with your right and left forefingers. The tapping indicates "I know that information and can retrieve it easily."

COMPREHENSION: Hold the sides of your head to denote "My brain understands and can find the information quickly."

APPLICATION: Pantomime painting the sides of your legs, knees to waist to indicate "When I do something with (apply) the information, I understand it much better."

ANALYSIS: Pantomime looking through a microscope and adjusting the lens to see the subject better. This motion suggests "If I look closely, I can analyze the components, or parts, of the information."

SYNTHESIS: As a magician would, roll your fists one over the other three times and finish with arms extended at shoulder height, exclaiming, "Voilà!" This motion (typically students' favorite) denotes "I can put it all together so it has meaning!"

EVALUATION: Assume a posture of contemplation in the spirit of Rodin's *Thinker.* Rest your chin in one hand, supporting it with your other hand if you are standing or your knee if you're sitting. This pose symbolizes "I can weigh both sides of an issue and arrive at an informed conclusion."

Becky expected that by the end of the lesson, students would be able to apply the levels to a range of questions and, ultimately, write questions for each other using selected picture books that had been distributed as content resources.

Let's start with the first term—*value*. Students placed an emotional value on the highly interactive procedure they followed to learn the six levels. Becky had students stand at their desks and asked them to start walking when they heard music and stop when the music stopped. Shortly after the music began and students had begun to move around the room, Becky stopped the music and showed students a gesture that would help them recall the first level of the taxonomy. "Knowledge," Becky declared as she tapped her forehead, "is what we know in our head, so the picture and movement you should have in your brain is tapping your head." The music started again and students resumed walking around the room. When the music stopped again, Becky told them that the motion for the comprehension level of the taxonomy was cradling your head in your hands, suggesting that the information is right there, in the brain, ready to be accessed. The class learned gestures for the next three levels following the same procedure. (See page 17 for all six gestures.)

Having multiple reinforcements and being fully engaged as learners helps us store new information in our memory system. In this case, Becky encouraged the *storage* of the information in the brain's hippocampus through rehearsing the six levels three times in taxonomic sequence and then three times randomly with the music.

Coherence occurs when all learning goals for the lesson connect to form a meaningful whole. Our brains strive to extract meaning from the world around us; coherence is when it all comes together. Becky's students developed coherence by using familiar books to practice writing original questions based on the six levels. To show that their memories of the taxonomy had become coherent, the students shared these questions with the class, and the class tried to identify the level of each.

Not only did students master the six levels over the course of the lesson, they were able to retrieve the information with nearly perfect accuracy on a quiz three weeks later. In this way, Becky and the host teacher could be sure that students had effectively stored a coherent understanding of the six levels of Bloom's Taxonomy in their long-term memories, an understanding they would be asked to use in lessons throughout the year.

MOVING TOWARD LONG-TERM MEMORY

What else do teachers need to know about memory? In addition to considering how students will value, store, and make sense of the ideas and information they learn, we also need to look at the three levels of the memory system and how students can commit key learning to their long-term memory.

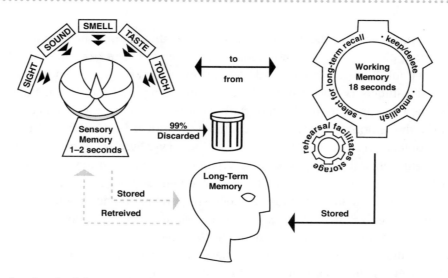

The first level of the memory system is *sensory memory*. The information absorbed at this level is anything that comes across our personal radar screen via touch, sight, sound, smell, or taste at a given moment. In a classroom, sensory distractions are everywhere. A child's cough, lights that are too bright, an uncomfortable chair, the sound of a book dropped on the floor, or the smell of pizza drifting in from the cafeteria may all register briefly as blips on a student's mental radar screen. On occasion, some highly stimulating visual memory stimulus will pass directly into long-term memory (Smith, 2005), but 99 percent of sensory data does not even pass through to working memory and, thus, is discarded. The challenge to teachers is to make sure that the information students need to know remains, as part of the 1 percent retained in the memory system.

Working memory, part of the executive function of the prefrontal cortex, helps us remember moment to moment (Smith, 2005). As new information is taught, working memory is activated. When a student learns new content, this information must travel through his or her working memory "gateway" before moving into long-term memory.

In the brain, the function of working memory is to hold information temporarily and then determine what portion of it will be deleted, embellished, or selected. The process of moving from working memory to long-term memory requires our brains to determine whether to:

- Keep this information or discard it as unnecessary (*keep or delete*)

- Accept as accurate and incorporate new information with information already known about this topic (*embellish,* or *add to existing information*)

- Hold on to this new information for future use (*select for long-term recall*)

How does the decision-making process pertaining to *keep or delete* work? If a student becomes overwhelmed with the amount of content presented at one time, he or she may delete important pieces of the lesson because of the overload. The newly presented content may be deleted for other reasons, as well. Perhaps the way the information is conveyed is tedious—or the student is daydreaming about the upcoming weekend. When students lose portions of the content or are unable to absorb what is being taught, coherence is threatened because the information has gaps and cannot be retrieved for meaning. These two examples—content overload and "bored to death"—show why it is critical to know about memory systems when designing lessons; a strong lesson can avoid the pitfalls of traditional teacher-directed lessons, namely, too much content and boring delivery.

Now let's look at the idea of embellishment—responding to and integrating new learning with information we already know. This embellishing process can both help and hinder comprehension and long-term memory building. As it receives information, a student's brain may introduce confirming evidence or inaccuracies about the content, which may clarify the concepts being taught or garble them completely.

On one hand, embellishing can accelerate information's transition to long-term memory if substantial prior knowledge exists and new connections reinforce preexisting fledgling synapses. For example, if a student's independent project focuses on the 1906 San Francisco earthquake and its impact on structures in the city, the student's prior knowledge is likely to embellish the content of a science lesson on earthquakes.

On the other hand, embellishing can create confusion and unresolved dissonance in students' learning. In a lesson on the prehistoric era, for example, a student might be presented with information about dinosaurs and may vividly recall an animated movie in which dinosaurs behave in a way that is contrived and unrealistic. Such a false picture can bring misinformation to the current lesson and distort the content. The potential for students to internalize the wrong information is one reason teachers need to provide opportunities for regular, meaningful feedback. Teachers must check students' understanding of content to ensure that they are not learning faulty information.

When we teach and review new information, our hope, of course, is that the intended content will be *selected* and accurately directed to long-term memory. The good news is that since most sensory memory data is discarded or forgotten, students aren't overwhelmed with perpetual trivial pursuits. The bad news is that if teachers do not create lessons that ensure that the specific content to be learned

Embellishing

In creative thinking, embellishing can be meaningful. For example, in a problem-solving task, a student may present original ideas by elaborating on existing solutions.

travels through the working memory gateway into long-term memory, students might end up discarding the information they need to know.

Checking for Understanding

Checking for understanding is a key to helping students know when they have truly learned something. Try these three strategies:

1. Have students use color-coded highlighters to self-assess at the end of a lesson or at given points during the week's instruction. They can highlight notes as follows:

    green = I know the content and can explain it to another student or the teacher.

    yellow = I remember a few things about the content but need some review.

    red = I need to hear the information again—and maybe in a new way—to understand it.

2. At intervals in the lesson, you can ask students to respond on their own or with a partner to one of the following questions:

    If you were the teacher explaining the two most important pieces of information from this text (mini-lecture, study guide) what would you tell the class?

    Draw a T-chart in your notes (or on scratch paper). On the left, write down two or three things you are confident that you know; on the right, write two or three things you need to understand better.

    What do you need to do next if you are not sure of information that was taught today?

3. As a closure activity, give a "Getting the Facts" true/false student-developed quiz. Hand out two sheets of scratch paper to each student. Have students write one T/F question on each sheet, based on the lesson of the day. Put the questions in a basket and have each student select one. Have students answer the question they selected and say why it is true or false. Variation: If a student gets a question he or she doesn't want, the student can ask someone else to answer, but then he or she must answer that person's question or select another question.

New content does not sit around in working memory. Working memory has a life of approximately 18 seconds unless the new information "hooks on" to something a student already knows. A neuron activated by the new information searches to make a connection to an existing network of neurons for learning to become more permanent (Wolfe, 2001).

Thus, when new information hooks to prior knowledge, synapses are reinforced or new ones are created.

PROCEDURAL AND DECLARATIVE MEMORY

We've considered the memory system from the perspective of sensory memory and long-term memory. Within the long-term memory system, scientists describe a two-part system. There is *procedural memory*—unconscious or automatic systems, such as driving a car—and *declarative memory*—conscious systems of knowing facts and locating information (Sylwester, 2005). Procedural memory relates to the recall of a process or series of steps that are generally carried out in sequence and usually involve motor or kinesthetic responses. Procedural memory activates neurons in the basal ganglia and cerebellum, which have oversight of motor and conditioned responses (Smith, 2005; Wolfe, 2001). In short, procedural memory pertains to *how* things are done.

Procedural Memory

The purpose of procedural memory is for the student to become very efficient at tasks that need to be performed routinely. These are tasks we do not want to reteach constantly or have students relearn constantly. For example, when my daughter received her driver's permit, I wanted her to become very efficient at the basic skills of driving so that she would not have to think about every turn, every movement of the vehicle; I wanted these skills to become the solid foundation upon which she would base her additional learning. I knew that if she learned the basics of driving implicitly, she could then pay more attention to the ever-changing road environment and, in turn, become a safer, more confident driver.

Similarly, coaches want their players to get certain procedures down automatically. You'll hear them say, "Don't think about it—just do it!" Three-point shots in basketball, the art of goaltending in soccer, the moves of a cheerleader—all relate to procedural recall. The coach wants the players to perform efficiently at a higher skill level, which in turn will elevate the performance of the individual and team.

Students want to know the systems they are expected to follow and the level at which they are expected to perform. In many ways, these procedures help students settle in to the culture of their classrooms or school and pave the way for learning "the important stuff." Here are some classroom routines that draw on procedural memory:

✔ Bell work at the beginning of class

✔ Interactive note-taking steps

✔ Science lab safety measures

✔ Collecting homework

✔ Rules for cooperative groups

✔ Cafeteria lunch-line processes

✔ Procedures for assemblies

✔ Fire drills

Procedural memory is enhanced with review and practice. To make their expectations clear, teachers often post procedural steps on the classroom walls, including fire drill procedures, rules for turning in homework, classroom rules, and stages of problem solving. Procedural memory is also at work during literacy instruction when students follow steps in a writer's workshop or a vocabulary lesson.

Literacy Strategy Taps Procedural Memory

Procedural memory is activated when students use a literacy strategy, such as a QAR (question-answer/relationship) task, which outlines specific procedures to use when thinking about a passage from a textbook or story:

- The first QAR strategy, Right There, suggests that the answer is within a single sentence and the reader will have no problem finding it.

- The second strategy, Think and Search, informs the reader that the answer is in the text but must be sought out by the reader.

- The third QAR strategy, On My Own, represents a question that can be answered from the reader's background knowledge or personal connection to the text.

- The fourth QAR, Writer and Me, is an interpretive question that draws upon the reader's background knowledge and inferences from the text (Raphael, 1986).

Declarative Memory

Declarative memory is activated when students learn new information or new content. Procedural memory concentrates on *how*; declarative memory focuses on *what*—specifically, what students need to know to meet learning goals and pass required assessments. Declarative memory encompasses both episodic memory and semantic memory.

EPISODIC MEMORY

Location, location, location! How often has it been said that a great real estate deal depends on location? Episodic memory is also driven by location. Our brains remember experiences branded by time and place with enhanced recall if there is a high level of emotion surrounding the experience. Go back to that memory of the best vacation you've ever had and consider again a time, place, and picture in your mind. These memories can often be readily retrieved. Childhood memories of staying at grandma's house, a week spent in Cancún, or a trip to the Grand Canyon may be easy to recall,

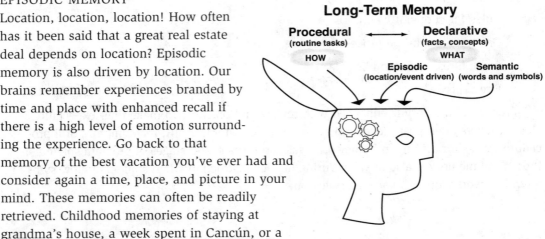

Long-Term Memory

but unfortunately, so are unpleasant experiences. One vivid recollection I have is of when I was 7 years old, vacationing with my parents and siblings in a rustic cabin on an island in the middle of a lake in Canada—with spiders in the outhouse! Regardless of whether an experience is positive or negative, episodic memory is activated when we remember an event and the details surrounding that event.

How does episodic memory manifest itself in the classroom? One example comes from a third-grade teacher who told me that prior to giving a social studies test, she had covered up a bulletin board with information about the Lewis and Clark expedition—content that was on the test. During the test, she saw students turn to the bulletin board as if they were seeing the hidden pictures. Episodic memory also may be enhanced when a teacher uses color to cue certain responses. For example, when working with root words and affixes, it is helpful to always write the root words in black, prefixes in red, and suffixes in green, so when a student sees a word in black, he or she recognizes immediately that it is a root word.

Episodic memory is enhanced when teachers use props to accentuate. For example:

- Use unique hats to identify historical figures
- Use masks to depict personality traits of a character
- Read poems with a prop related to the author, time period, or style of poem, such as using a top hat à la the *Cat in the Hat* for Dr. Seuss books

Change the location of the lesson. For example:

- Move the math measurement lesson to the outside courtyard

- Teach from the back of the room instead of the front
- Change desks around for a specific lesson or unit of study so students associate a desk configuration with content ("I remember that our desks were in a circle in a Socratic Seminar when we discussed that story.")

Use color to highlight aspects of the lesson. For example:

- Use study guides in different colors for different subjects (science notes in a yellow binder, math in a blue binder, and so on)
- Designate specific colors for the parts of speech on word walls

Provide experiences associated with content. For example:

- Reenact a Civil War battle with paper-wad ammunition on the field
- Role-play the signing of the Declaration of Independence

SEMANTIC MEMORY

Semantic memory stores definitions, facts, figures, and information that isn't tied to experience. It is activated when students are asked to remember the names and attributes of geometric shapes in math, parts of speech in language arts, or the countries of South America. All students learn that George Washington was the first president of the United States. A trip to his home in Mount Vernon, Virginia, might reinforce information about Washington's life, but the fact that he was the first president must simply be memorized. The bottom line is that much of what students are expected to learn in school involves semantic memory.

The key to successful activation of semantic memory is rehearsal. New information that is to be learned must be reinforced through repetition over a period of time. A good curriculum pacing guide that outlines the scope and sequence of the subject area will include rehearsal of content so that students keep reinforcing the connections that are being wired in the brain.

Avoid a "Just-the-Facts" Mind-set

Across the nation, students at all grade levels are responsible for learning countless discrete facts and figures. In fact, with so much weight placed on test taking, the standards movement is often criticized for reducing education to the point where students are forced to learn pieces of information just to spit back on a test. Many teachers compensate for a "just-the-facts" mind-set by consciously designing lessons that tie the required factual information to "big ideas" that build conceptual understandings.

Mirror Neurons: Why Modeling Is So Important

Mirror neurons came to the attention of Italian researchers in the early 1990s, when they identified specific neurons in the brains of macaque monkeys that fired not only when the monkeys grabbed a specific object, but when they *watched* another monkey—or human, for that matter—grab the same object (Winerman, 2005). A similar thing occurs when one little league player is watching another at bat. The seated child's brain mirrors the brain of the child at bat—both are anticipating the pitch and the swing to follow.

Similarly, since neurons that fire together wire together, a student's synaptic connections can become stronger—and, in turn, more permanent—by observing a teacher doing a task. A question pertaining to mirror neurons that teachers might ask is: Do I model procedures and think-alouds sufficiently for students to activate mirror neurons, thereby helping students rehearse content to be learned?

Mirror neurons respond when we observe emotion, as well. For example, you may have talked to colleagues or friends facing hardships and found tears running down your face in empathy. We now know that similar areas of the brain are activated for both the person experiencing the emotion and the person commiserating: Mirror neurons are at work when we internalize the emotional state of others by observing their facial expressions, body language, and actions. If we expect students to behave compassionately and thoughtfully, then we need to show them genuine models of caring relationships with adults and peers.

What is critical to understand is that activating mirror neurons can have a beneficial effect on your instruction and the experiences of your students.

A Teacher's Job: Developing Long-Term Memory

As a teacher, how does knowledge of memory systems affect the planning and delivery of instruction? If teachers respond to the following questions prior to the lesson, the teaching experience should be meaningful for both the student and teacher.

- Do I know the learning goals for students recommended by my curriculum and/or pacing guides?
- Have I considered which of the specific goals of the lesson involve procedural and/or declarative memory tasks?

- Have I planned how I will teach procedures embedded in the lesson?

- Have I built in time for rehearsal of the procedures?

- Have I identified strategies to build declarative memory to help students learn the facts, figures, information, and content of the learning goals?

- Do I know when and how I will model for students both practice and metacognitive thinking (think-alouds), keeping mirror-neuron activation in mind?

- Have I determined a way to assess whether students remember what is taught?

- Have I anticipated how I will reinforce the learning goals from today's lesson *tomorrow*?

Understanding the memory system is an important first step for teachers. Like our students, we must become conversant in how the brain really learns and consider how our students will best remember the content we teach. Once you've internalized this information, you will be on your way to developing brain-compatible lessons. As you continue to the next chapter, you will learn how to craft powerful lessons for optimal student learning.

Reflection

1. It is important to observe the memory processes of your students. In this chapter, we discussed how students may delete, embellish, or select information during the transition from working memory to long-term memory. Please answer the following questions.

   - How do you know if a student has deleted the information you want him or her to learn before that student misses it on the test?

   - Can you give an example of an occasion where a student embellished the content so much that the meaning was compromised?

2. Think about procedural, episodic, and semantic memory. Write at least two examples of each type of memory that was in use in your classroom in the last few weeks.

3. Use the Internet to research the role of the hippocampus in forming memories. Write three to five insights that you have gained.

4. **ACTIVATING PRIOR KNOWLEDGE (APK):** Recall what you believe to be the most effective lesson you've delivered to students. Outline at least five reasons why you think the lesson worked so well. APK activities will help prime your brain for what's ahead!

Chapter 3

DESIGNER'S CHALLENGE:
Lesson Design, That Is!

A NUMBER OF television shows highlight the importance of quality design—from maximizing the use of color and texture to the optimal use of space. These design programs help viewers consider whether to use an eclectic mix of materials or stick with one style. They even present ways to economize and design "on a dime." I'm particularly impressed with a show that transforms an entire room in a weekend (and wouldn't mind if agents of the show were to arrive on my doorstep!). In some ways, implementing quality lesson design is not terribly different—a teacher has to use materials, resources, space, and time in a variety of combinations to find the best instruction for a classroom of students. Thus, our journey to teach smarter with the brain in focus continues with how-to guidance on lesson design.

Let's start by having you read the statements below and decide whether they are mostly true (T) or false (F).

T OR F	STATEMENTS
	1. I consistently teach the learning targets that are outlined in the curriculum pacing guides.
	2. The assessments I use with students indicate that they consistently meet the learning targets.
	3. I regularly design lessons that differentiate for both remedial and enrichment students in my classroom.
	4. I activate my students' prior knowledge at the beginning of each new lesson, across all subject areas.
	5. I consistently use strategies that actively engage students as learners.
	6. I avoid "telling" and require students to do the thinking.

You've just completed an advanced organizer. Work by Marzano et al. asserts that the use of advanced organizers correlates with improvement in student achievement (2001).

Although responses to this advanced organizer differ from reader to reader, I find that most teachers struggle in several, if not all, of the areas cited above. A significant word in these statements is *consistently*. One teacher told me, "I differentiate sometimes, but not consistently." Another teacher ruefully responded, "I do a great job with activating prior knowledge in literacy and social studies, but APK just falls to the wayside when it comes to math!"

Responding to the statement "I avoid 'telling' and require students to do the thinking" also brings a grimace from outstanding teachers. How effective are we at consistently encouraging students as thinkers? How many opportunities to draw out the thinking of students do we miss in every lesson? I recently observed a language arts teacher give a thorough and insightful critique of the poem she had just read aloud to students, explaining to them—in 15 minutes' worth of extensive detail—what it was all about. I asked her in our after-lesson follow-up, "Who did most of the work of interpreting the poem—you or your students?" She knew immediately what had happened, "You're so right—I told them my interpretation and barely got them to talk!" In her case, students weren't doing the thinking—she was. Once she realized this, she made it very clear that next time she would develop the lesson so her students would be doing the work. If many of us—like this well-intentioned, proficient teacher—struggle with putting all the components of quality lesson design together, how can we coach ourselves and each other to address these concerns?

It's in the Lesson Design

In order to design brain-compatible lessons that can help transform classroom instruction, we have to look closely at our planning routines and the decisions we make about instruction. When I started teaching, my principal required teachers to put lesson plans for the upcoming week on his desk by 3:30 each Friday afternoon. These plans were in a table format with the times of day as rows and the days of the week as columns. I had a 1-by-2-inch space for each period, in which to write the textbook or workbook name, page number, and whether it was small-group or whole-group teaching. And that was it—lesson plans complete!

I wish I could say the days of lesson-plan minimalism are over, but I know that too many teachers still consider these brief notations to be a sufficient reminder of what they need to teach. The assertion "We're professionals, and experienced teachers don't need to have a detailed outline; new teachers, maybe, but not teachers who've been in the classroom a while" reveals a mind-set that can seriously undermine the effectiveness of instruction for students; even the best teachers falter if they don't plan daily for student achievement. The teachers in classrooms with bell-to-bell learning plan extensively.

Imagine you're putting together a dinner party for ten guests. You have many details to consider: buffet or sit-down, any allergies or food aversions, relatives or friends that shouldn't sit next to each other? And the menu—is it balanced with proteins, greens, and carbs? Finally, the culminating event—what dessert is the perfect capstone for the meal? Preparing for each day in a classroom is like planning an engaging menu for students. A teacher examines the diversity of the students and the content to be taught and asks: Who should or should not sit next to each other? Which small group of students will most effectively complete a cooperative learning task? What adjustments should be made for the students who are struggling readers? How can I regroup the students based on the assessment I gave on Friday? Which strategies should I use to make sure students are engaged? What exit activity will encourage retention of content taught that day?

Four Rules for Powerful Lesson Design

Designing a quality learning experience for students is the very first step of effective teaching. These four principles of lesson design are important to consider prior to delivering instruction:

1. Identify the essential knowledge to be learned and method(s) of assessment and feedback.

2. Activate prior knowledge to build connections to new content.

3. Select a variety of strategies to engage all learners.

4. Teach bell-to-bell and provide closure.

Through these rules may seem quite straightforward, framing the lesson design components in the context of brain-based learning brings new insight to the process.

LESSON DESIGN RULE 1:
IDENTIFY ESSENTIAL KNOWLEDGE TO BE LEARNED

Identifying the essential knowledge to be learned has several embedded assumptions:

• Within a curriculum map and/or pacing guide, the *what* of the content to be taught is defined.

• Effective tools of assessment inform the teacher about achievement levels and serve as the basis for differentiated instruction.

In most curriculum guides, content is frequently outlined with an overarching objective stated first, followed by specific topics displayed in a bulleted format. "Teaching to the bullet" means that a specific sub-objective in the curriculum or learning standards is expected to be taught—usually within a designated time period. Most of us are held accountable for very specific content targets that will be assessed on standardized or criterion-referenced state tests, so we have no choice but to know what they are and to make sure we teach them in ways that will help all students succeed. Unfortunately, these tests tend to embody a one-size-fits-all mind-set.

Assessing students for the purpose of differentiating instruction according to their identified needs is the second assumption. This concept of differentiation—using a wide array of assessments—is central to brain-compatible instructional design. When a teacher differentiates, he or she recognizes that each learner brings a range of unique background experiences to a learning task. Because students' brains have different levels of preparation for learning, effective differentiation depends on our ability to assess with clarity, design targeted lessons based on this wide array of ongoing assessments (both formative and summative), and adapt content and processes to teach and reteach as needed.

The imperative "begin with the end in mind" embraces the concept of backward design (Wiggins & McTighe, 1998), which indicates that we should align content and assessment *before* we deliver instruction. Including strategies that familiarize students with the way in which the material is tested is also important. For example, if the standard states that "the student will demonstrate knowledge of how economic decisions are made in the marketplace by comparing the differences among free market, command, and mixed economies" (Virginia Standards of Learning, Civics, and Economics 9.b, 7th grade), then, quite sensibly, students should have practice in comparing and contrasting these economies. Teaching content in the way it will be assessed creates more connections in the brain, reinforcing the growth of synapses.

Varying Assessments Is Brain-Savvy

Teachers should keep in mind that it is essential to provide feedback to students using a variety of assessment methods. Typically, a test administered statewide is constructed as a summative, selected-response test. *Summative* means that it is administered at the end of a grading period or school term. *Selected-response* refers to multiple-choice or fill-in-the-blank tests, which are much easier to score than performance-based or portfolio assessments. Although students should practice the format of formal state tests to become test-savvy, they need to experience a variety of ongoing (formative) assessments using clearly stated criteria or rubrics. These assessments make clear what the teacher expects them to learn and do, and provide students with a stronger grasp of the content they need to know for the summative test.

Is there a difference between aligning instruction with assessment and teaching to the test? An analogy might help explain the distinction. Aligning instruction and assessment is like a homebound ship on an open sea with a number of options for reaching the port; teaching to the test is a boat in a system of canal locks—constricted with tight boundaries. Both arrive in port—yet, during the journey, the learning experiences are very different.

Selecting Teaching Resources With Differentiation in Focus

I've noted that one of the greatest dilemmas in content-area instruction—particularly in upper elementary and middle school—occurs when teachers adhere strictly to the textbook. For some reason, as students get older, teachers frequently, and sometimes exclusively, use the text as the course sequence and primary resource. Having worked in a school system where one out of four students entering the sixth grade read two or more years behind grade level, I know that it is essential to rely on resources other than the content textbook.

Even if a teacher has a clear grasp of "teaching to the bullet" with alignment of content and assessment, the entire instructional effort will break down if the textbook is three grade levels too difficult for one-third of the class. The life-science teacher who is using only the seventh-grade science text to teach cell structure runs the risk of losing a third of the class simply because the book is at a frustration reading level for many students.

Nonfiction leveled trade books support differentiated instruction. I once observed an eighth-grade physical science teacher teaching about magnetism. To supplement the eighth-grade science text, she found two sets of books on magnetism in the literacy library—one at a sixth-grade level and one at a fourth-grade level. Each of the books contained the concepts and key vocabulary about magnetism that were outlined in the curriculum pacing guide. The teacher set up centers with questions for students to answer, as well as mini-experiments using the different books as information sources and the textbook as a reference. The centers were differentiated based on reading levels, but since the tasks were similar, the variations in reading levels were not obvious to the students.

A good way to reduce your reliance on a single text is by making leveled content-area books available to your students. The ideal literacy-rich classroom should provide students with opportunities to become familiar with the points of view of numerous authors. I am a strong proponent of using picture books with upper elementary and middle school students. Imagine the thinking and literacy skills that could be developed if older students were to take a science picture book on a theme, for example, "predator and prey," and write a scientifically based text for it. Enriching content instruction in this way, by moving beyond the single text, offers limitless possibilities.

Helping Students Understand Differentiation

Christy Davis, elementary school teacher and instructional coach, shares how she helps students understand differentiation: "As my teaching career progressed, so did my realization that one size does not fit all. I needed to find a way to communicate this understanding to my students. That's when Dr. Davis became my alter ego. Every year on the first day of school, I don my lab coat, stethoscope, and funny glasses with the big nose, and give cue cards to three students who assist me by playing patients in a silly skit. One at a time, they come up to me. One complains of an earache, another has a tummy ache, and the last has a sprained ankle. Regardless of the complaint, I prescribe the same thing: I pretend to squirt drops in their ears, stick in a cotton ball, hand them a breath mint 'pill,' and tell them to call me in a week.

"Then I ask, 'Did these patients receive the care they needed?' Students laugh. 'No way!' A classroom is a lot like medical care. Each student has a unique mix of needs, strengths, and learning characteristics, and not everyone requires the same treatment. I explain to them that there will be times when they will not be doing the same activity as their classmates, but they will be doing what is best for them. I even created a prescription pad to write individual assignments from Dr. Davis. In the years that I've used this approach, students have accepted specific assignments without question. Differentiation has been possible because the children understand it is in their best interest."

LESSON DESIGN RULE 2: MAKE CONNECTIONS

As teachers, we want students to make connections between information they already have in their brains—existing neurons—and the new information we're teaching them. When those connections are strong, we can help them activate prior knowledge quickly and effectively. "Tagging" learning experiences with sensory and emotional cues is a powerful way to do that.

We learned in Chapter 2 that when we are presented with new content, the brain searches for an existing framework of neurons to which it can attach this new information, thus creating sensory memories. Introducing concepts with colors, shapes, art, rhymes, music, textures, and even flavors and scents, when appropriate, can be powerful ways to help students link key information to existing memories. Chapters 4, 5, and 6 suggest more ways to tap the senses.

Aromatic Memories

Have you ever marveled at the way your olfactory sense—the sense of smell—can immediately evoke vivid memories? A few years ago, when I walked into a bakery where blueberry pies had just been taken out of the oven, not only did I recall my mother making blueberry pies in our farm kitchen, but I immediately pictured our family going to pick blueberries on the mountaintop and filling milk pails full of the ripe berries. In short, my brain experienced deep connections of present to past . . . and I bought a pie!

As Becky Morehouse's lesson in Chapter 2 showed, placing an emotional value on learning is one way to ensure that the information is processed and stored. When one of my colleagues needed her students to identify the key geography of Southeast Asia, she decided to use a current news topic—the tsunami of December 2004—to help. A doctor friend of mine had spent two months on a Mercy Ship, providing medical care to the victims, and we invited her to speak about her experiences to the eighth-grade students. Her pictures and stories were the connectors that helped them understand the culture, people, and geography of the region. Though the students had little awareness of the geography of Southeast Asia, they were able to understand and meet the geography content standards inherent in her discussion because the visiting doctor's poignant stories served as a rich reference point. We know that when memories are "tagged" with emotion, they can be retrieved more readily. Students referred to this doctor's visit many times in the weeks that followed—and demonstrated enhanced recall because of the emotional tag to the experience.

Connection-Building Strategies

Helping students make connections by activating prior knowledge needs to be planned for, but does not have to be time-consuming or complicated. The following strategies to activate prior knowledge require minimal planning and can readily be incorporated into a lesson design:

- **PREDICT/SUPPORT PREREADING STRATEGY:** If you are planning to use a selection from a text or resource book, have students look over the pages to be covered. Ask questions such as "What do the pictures, graphs, or boxes tell you about this section?" and "Based on the headings and subheadings of this portion of the text, what do you think the main points of this section will be about?" Another approach is to ask students to read several key paragraphs in an introductory portion of the text and predict something that they might learn based on what they've read. After a student has made a prediction, ask, "Can you please read the sentence or section of the text that supports your prediction?" This follow-up question ensures that students are drawing from the evidence presented in the text.

- **BRAINSTORMING:** Brainstorming prompts, such as "Tell me anything you can think of that has to do with volcanoes," are frequently used to activate prior knowledge. The main drawback of brainstorming is that teachers end up calling on the two or three students who volunteer, while the rest of the class is just waiting for the teacher to move on. Rather than using the whole-group what-do-you-know-about approach, give students a "think page" (a half-sheet of scratch paper) and ask them to write two or three things on their own before you take responses from the whole group. This approach to brainstorming will generate more responses and keep all learners tuned in. Additionally, writing responses on an overhead or whiteboard is more effective than just taking the oral response because the written record taps into oral and visual learning styles and reinforces additional learning modalities.

- **WEBBING OR MIND-MAPPING:** Prior to a unit of study on, for example, why George Washington is known as the father of our country, have students create a web of information they can remember about George Washington. (If students are not familiar with a web format, model the web technique with something they know well—for example, try webbing everything that comes to mind about basketball.) A mind-map is 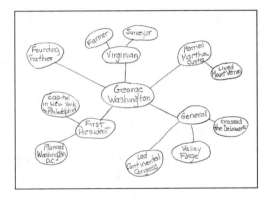 similar to a web but it uses pictures, images, or icons to enhance recall.

- **GRAPHIC ORGANIZERS:** Although webs and mind-maps can be categorized as graphic organizers, a number of other formats exist as resources for teachers to use to help students structure their own learning. In *Teaching Reading: A Complete Resource for Grades 4 and Up*, Laura Robb offers an array of graphic organizers that support literacy (2006). Additionally, software designed to enable students to create graphic organizers, such as Inspiration and Kidspiration, is available in many classrooms. When selecting a graphic organizer, it is important for a teacher to match it to the thinking task(s) required of students. We'll look more closely at ways to effectively use graphic organizers and provide additional examples in Chapter 4.

- **A-TO-Z REVIEW:** In this strategy, students write down any word, phrase, name, date, city, or other piece of information that relates to a given subject using the letters of the alphabet as a prompt. The A-to-Z format is also effective as a closure activity. An A-to-Z review completed by individual students provides valuable preassessment information. Students also enjoy doing this organizer in pairs or triads; however, with partners, teachers should be careful about using this organizer as a diagnostic assessment because it may not reflect equal contributions from each student.

A to Z Review	
Appomattox	North
Bull Run	Open range fire
Confederate	Pickett
Destruction	Q
Emotional	Rebels
Fredricksburg	Surrender
Gettysburg	Torn soldiers
Horses	Under fire
Infantry	V
Jackson	Washington DC
Killing	X
Little Round Top	Yankees
Malitia	Z

Name: _____ Date: 5/24/07
Topic: Civil War
_X_ Pre ___ Post ___ Individual ___ Partner ___ Group

- **PICTURE PROMPTS:** We know that picture prompts and other nonverbal representations help students hold onto information. Recently, I taught a U.S. history class for several class periods. The content I had to cover focused on the Industrial Revolution and the rise of social consciousness. On a Web site, I found photographs from the time period showing child laborers' brutal work conditions and tenement housing. I also found photographs of contemporary sweatshops in developing countries and examples of present-day housing. I used the first photographs to get students to reflect on why social consciousness emerged in the past century; I brought out the second set of photographs after students responded to the question, "Are these conditions present today?" The pictures helped students make connections to the topic, and encouraged their "buy in" to the lesson.

- **WRITE/DRAW-SHARE:** Even if you have already introduced a topic in a previous class, it is still important to activate prior knowledge. Asking students to write or draw three things that they can recall from the previous day's class can help them make those connections. Having a student share those responses with another student allows for interaction and conversation. In the final step in this variation on Think-Pair-Share, students share responses with the whole class while the teacher records the feedback.

- **CONSTRUCT A QUESTION:** In this strategy, students review lessons from the previous day (or days) through the task of writing a test question. A teacher might introduce it to students like this: "Yesterday, we talked about cloud formations and the weather associated with these formations. Working alone or with one other person, write one question that I could include on the unit post-test scheduled for Friday. Please use a multiple-choice format today. You may refer to your notes."

- **ADVANCED ORGANIZERS:** We began this chapter with an advanced organizer. The rationale for the technique is that it activates prior knowledge and provides a purpose for reading if applied properly. Advanced organizers are typically developed using a true/false format. The teacher tells students "Read the questions and write a 'T' if you think the statement is true and an 'F' if you think the statement is false. If you do not know, it is okay to guess. Remember it is not what you know; rather, what you *think* you might know. I won't provide the answers until the end of the lesson, but as we move through the lesson, keep your ears and eyes open for answers."

LESSON DESIGN RULE 3: ENGAGE LEARNERS

Keeping learners engaged in a classroom can be very tricky. Some teachers rule with an iron fist, either because they are apprehensive about what students will do if given any freedom or because they themselves were ruled with an iron fist, and thus the cycle of restrictive teaching is perpetuated. I worry that learners in these kinds of classes will only be marginally engaged at best. In another type of classroom, other teachers assign numerous interactive activities to keep students continuously involved, but the activities are weak and ill-focused, so these classrooms end up centers of busywork, where genuine engagement is minimal. When we create the conditions for students to become engaged in our lessons and apply brain-compatible principles throughout instruction, we can ensure that students are focused, interested, and learning. (Additional discussion about engaging learners will be highlighted in Chapter 6.)

The Time Factor

Time is the first variable to manipulate when it comes to engaging students in the classroom. We know that our brains employ a focus/refocus approach to learning (Jensen, 1995). When a teacher intently zeroes in on specific content to be learned, it is important to let the students' brains work on that content for a while before being given even more information to absorb. For example, allowing students to work on a section of a study guide or graphic organizer following a portion of a lecture is more effective than having them do the on-your-own work after the full lecture.

The M-capacity—defined as the number of mental representations, such as dates, names, locations, or terms, that a person can keep activated in working memory (Pascual-Leone & Baillargeon, 1994)—provides additional rationale for chunking lessons so that students have more frequent opportunities to focus/refocus. Studies have shown that the number of items that can be held in working memory varies with age (Wolfe, 2001). Very simply, if too much information is crammed into the brain without a chance for processing, much of the content will be pushed out or deleted. Have you ever been bowling when too many bowling balls are returning to the tray? The balls returning have no place to go, unless someone picks up a ball. Similarly, if too much content is pushed into students' brains, the new content has no place to go—unless something taught earlier is dislodged to make room.

Teachers often wonder how long they can keep the attention of students during an instructional task. One suggested guide is to consider the student's age, then add or subtract two minutes (Jensen, 1995, p. 56.) Let me share how I explain to middle school teachers why sixth-grade classes are so unwieldy. Sixth graders are 12 years old. Using the age-plus-or-minus-two-minutes rule, a teacher should shift activities every 10–14 minutes. If the class is high risk, the shifts should be done every 10–12 minutes. Middle school teachers have a tendency to think in terms of 20- to 25-minute instructional sections, but these are simply too long for 12-year-old learners, and that's why their lessons fall short of keeping most students engaged.

M-CAPACITY	
AGE	
15	O O O O O O O
13	O O O O O O
11	O O O O O
9	O O O O
7	O O O
5	O O

O = Unit of information stored in working memory

M-capacity informs us that the amount of information students keep in their working memories increases with age.

I've challenged teachers to adjust lesson chunks for their middle school grades based on the age rule and have witnessed successes and received many testimonials that it works. One first-year teacher had complained, "I seem to get along with my students and they like my classes, but they just don't stay tuned in." He tried chunking his lessons based on the age guidelines, and within two weeks he reported a great difference in student engagement and attentiveness in class. "I am able to cover more content because I spend less time trying to get them to focus. On top of that, I am more successful at bell-to-bell teaching because the class energy level is higher and I can get more accomplished."

Please note that there can be exceptions to the age rule. Learners who are highly engaged and interested in the topic and have sufficient prior knowledge to generate connections can often focus for greater lengths of time. I have watched students sustain deep interest far beyond the age-plus-or-minus-two-minutes guide—though these occasions were generally instances of self-exploration and discovery and rarely the result of direct teaching. Unfortunately, students in a typical classroom frequently have little or no interest in the topics being discussed, and struggle to stay tuned in to the lesson.

The age-plus-or-minus-two-minutes guideline applies to all age levels. A first-grade teacher informed me that it helped her understand why her students got so restless during circle time. She explained, "My students are six years old, so I should have between four and eight minutes of focused time. I have some squirrelly students. I bring them to the rug,

Timing in a Lesson

If I am a sixth-grade social studies teacher preparing a 55-minute lesson on the Reconstruction following the Civil War, how might I apply what I know about the M-capacity and the age-plus-or-minus-two rule as I design my lesson? These self-reflections (at right) describe my lesson plan development:

UNIT GOAL: *Students will see the Civil War and Reconstruction as major turning points in American history.*

Lesson Targets	Time	Design Self-Reflections
Students need to understand the economic and social impact of the war and reconstruction.	4–5 min.	Rather than start off with a lecture, I will assess prior knowledge with an A-to-Z Review of everything they can recall about the post–Civil War period. I should be able to build on these responses since sixth graders have discussed the Civil War in fourth grade as well.
	8–10 min.	To set up the next task, I will ask students to make a T-chart in their social studies journals. On one side they should write a heading of "Economic Impact"; on the other side "Social Impact." At this point I will pair off students to keep them actively engaged. Combining their A-to-Z review responses, they are to write in the appropriate T-chart column any word or phrase that relates to either social or economic impact. I will provide 4–6 minutes for partner interaction. Then I will work with the whole group to compile a class list on the whiteboard.
	14 min.	From that information, in a mini-lecture I will confirm, expand upon, or modify some of the students' insights. Because of the M-capacity factor, I will limit my discussion to 4–5 "need-to-know" units of information about social and economic impacts.
		Also, since I want my students to regularly make connections to their world, I will tell them that I have a one-question filter for them to consider during the mini-lecture: "Think about what was happening in the United States during Reconstruction. Do similar conditions exist in today's world—locally, nationally, even globally?"
Students need to write reflections about the "filter question" and provide reasons.	8–10 min.	Students will write again in their social studies journals. The task this time will be to write about connections between our world today and the world of Reconstruction. I will model thinking: "I understand that during Reconstruction the former slaves embraced freedom, but at the same time, many did not know where to go or how to make a living away from the plantation. I wonder if people from Iraq seeking asylum in other countries have similar feelings of uncertainty about their futures?"

Lesson Targets	Time	Design Self-Reflections
Students will work in small groups and read sections from selected primary sources from the Reconstruction Web site.	12 min.	I will select a brief one- to two-paragraph section from three primary source documents, such as the Freedmen's Bureau Act 1865 or the First Reconstruction Act of 1867, all accessible at http://www.multied.com/documents/reconstruction.html. I will divide students into six small groups. (To ensure coverage of the text, groups 1 and 2 will have the same document; groups 3 and 4, the same; and groups 5 and 6, the same.) I will ask students to identify three main points and make connections to current events. They will write their key points on a blank transparency, with one person agreeing to present to the class. I will ask them to add pictures or images to help the class remember the content.
Students need to be reminded about important "need-to-know" content from the lesson in a closure activity.	6 min.	I will ask students to complete a 3, 2, 1 exit ticket and write down: • 3 things you learned today • 2 connections to today's world • 1 question for the teacher

have them sit in the square and start the activity. Around the fifth minute, the elbows start 'accidentally' making contact or the feet somehow tap an adjacent person—and my circle time begins to unravel. But if I have them stand up at minute 5 and get the wiggles out with a head-and-shoulders-knees-and-toes routine or some other movement and then have them sit down again, I can gain four to five more minutes of circle time!"

Novelty Engages Learners

Using novelty to improve recall and involve students is another tool for teachers in a brain-compatible classroom. When something is presented in a new and different way, the brain tunes in—causing *natural* stress levels to elevate. (Remember, a degree of stress is a good thing!) Under a perceived negative threat—if the information is confusing and doesn't make sense—cortisol may be released. If the content is perceived as interesting or challenging, adrenaline is released. Both these neurotransmitters act as memory fixatives (McGaugh, 2003). Teachers can capitalize on the fact that students' brains like novelty by providing students with new and different activities, which will help fix the content in their brains. Our attraction to things that are novel doesn't mean every lesson needs to be a dog-and-pony show—because then it would no longer be novel—but it does mean teachers should specifically plan for activity and engagement.

Other examples of building novelty into lesson design include:

- Introducing a lesson by bringing in an unusual prop or artifact, such as a black hat and broom to introduce Halloween poetry

- Creating opportunities for peer-teaching by having students coach one another as "experts" on a topic they have chosen from the unit of study you just finished

- Using M. C. Escher's *High and Low* (or any drawing that creates an optical illusion with merging spaces) as a metaphor for a literature selection with a theme of finding your way. Have students also consider the movable staircases depicted in the Harry Potter movies

- Changing the learner's state of engagement by moving from individual to cooperative group work, such as shifting from an at-your-desk journal writing activity to a peer-editing group

Camp Fractions: APK, Novelty, Relevance, and Differentiation

Camp Fraction is a novel, interactive unit created to engage fourth-grade students in using fractions in 'real-life' through a summer camp theme. Students are immediately drawn into the Camp Fraction environment when I—the counselor—arrive in the room wearing camper attire, complete with hat, whistle, and other props.

Students receive handbooks and complete an anticipation guide to record their feelings about specific skills involving fractions. Campers (students) and camp counselors (teachers) work together once or twice a week on a key concept involving fractions. Each lesson begins with an APK activity, then continues with the counselor modeling and campers practicing in small, differentiated work groups. Camping tools —such as technology, literature, and manipulatives—help campers transform abstract concepts into concrete understandings. Each camp session ends with a differentiated Camp Fraction challenge that provides closure for the current skill while at the same time reinforcing a previously taught skill. Campers are expected to answer the Camp Fraction challenge and explain their thought process in arriving at an answer.

In the last camp session, the campers revisit the anticipation guides they initially completed and it's amazing to see how their perceptions have deepened during the unit! Camp Fraction allows opportunities for risk-taking in a safe environment while rewarding small steps of success. There is never a dull day at Camp Fraction!

Tamara Letter, instructional coach

- Incorporating Readers Theater to review a lesson in social studies
- Demonstrating knowledge of content using nonverbal representations rather than written work, such as using only pictures and numbers to review a feature in the fifth-grade science book about the effects of the depletion of the Amazon rain forest
- Taking notes on the content using a 3-D graphic organizer, which involves a kinesthetic (hands-on) modality, such as the creation of a flip-book depicting the parts of a flower

Making Sure Lessons Are Brain Compatible

When I design a lesson, I keep the following guiding questions in mind to ensure that I engage my students:

- Do I need to differentiate the way I group certain students or use resources with them?
- Do I allocate time for my lesson activities based on students' age plus or minus two minutes?
- What are my higher-level questions and/or activities for this lesson?
- Do I have a variety of activities?
- Is there opportunity for some hands-on engagement?
- Am I conscious of "emotional amplitude" to grab the learners?
- Can I work in the use of nonverbal representations to capitalize on students' ability to remember pictures before I introduce text?
- Would music enhance this lesson?

Asking myself these questions doesn't mean that I cover each point every day in every class. If I use a music prompt today to help students remember the human body's skeletal system, I probably won't use it tomorrow (other than to review). However, asking these questions daily does mean that I design each lesson with a purpose. We will spend more time with activities that engage learners in the next chapters.

LESSON DESIGN RULE 4: TEACH BELL-TO-BELL

Prepare yourselves for a soapbox speech! I think we have a serious issue regarding bell-to-bell teaching. In my years in education, I have observed many teachers for a variety of reasons. I am concerned when we waste too much time. One way time is wasted is with ill-conceived "bell work." Bell work is review work assigned at the very beginning of class to get students settled and working as soon as they arrive—allowing teachers time for attendance. In one middle school social studies class, the bell work (writing key terms and their definitions in a notebook) went on for the first 15 minutes of class because not everyone had finished. I've seen bell work that is simply of no consequence—busywork that takes far too long. I do believe in bell-to-bell teaching, so if bell work is used, teachers need to make sure it is concise and relevant to the topic and can be stopped and reviewed quickly—even if everyone isn't done—so class can begin promptly.

I've also noticed that once class begins, time is lost with sidebar conversations—often begun by students in the middle of class, but at times furthered by the teacher. When a student says to a teacher, "I got my hair cut, did you notice?" the response should be "Later, let's focus on what we're doing," not a three-minute mini-discussion about haircuts. I observed another teacher set up an excellent partner activity based on a History Alive! unit, but as soon as he got the students started, one pupil interrupted, "Hey Coach, what did you think of the game last night?" The teacher, who coached the team, started a critique of the game. What did all the other students do? Stop and listen, of course. I don't mean to be stodgy about occasionally straying off task, but if it happens too often, much valuable time is lost.

Here are a few examples of focused five-minute bell work activities:

- On the overhead: Pick a term from the basket on the table. Draw three symbols or pictures that describe the term. Be prepared to explain the term to a partner in four minutes. You may look at your notes or book.

- On the board: Main characters in novels have flaws. Quickly find one or two examples of character flaws demonstrated by characters in the book you are reading. Be prepared to share the example and page with a partner in four minutes.

- On a bell-work slip: Read the following math word problem, but *do not* solve it. Write another similar problem, using a different context or story.

- On the board: We will be discussing westward expansion today. In four minutes, write as many words or phrases that you can think of related to the topic (at least ten). It is okay to guess. Examples: *Industrial Revolution, searching for a new life, uncertainty.*

Valuable time is also lost when a teacher decides to let students begin working on their homework at the end of class. Let's consider a sixth-grade middle school teacher on a 90-minute block schedule who looks at the clock and tells his students that they can work on homework for the last 15 minutes of class. Too often, what happens is that everyone attends to the homework for the first three to five minutes. Then a few students look up and begin whispering; a few more conversations begin and the noise picks up a bit. Another student begins talking to the teacher, getting her involved. Over the course of 15 minutes, two students studiously work on the homework while the others chitchat until the bell rings. The result is that for many of the students, ten minutes of class time has been lost.

A class like this just fizzles out. It is definitely not bell-to-bell teaching. There are times when it is appropriate for teachers to let students start homework in class—to check students' initial efforts and make sure they understand the assignment or to provide needed resources to complete the homework. However, in a 90-minute class, the homework monitoring should occur between the 70th and 80th minutes so the teacher can take back the last ten minutes of class for closure.

Meaningful Closure

The primacy/recency effect (Sousa, 2001) demonstrates that our brains tend to remember what happens first and what happens last, so class should begin with clear statements about what will happen on that day, and the end of class should have closure. The last thing students should hear before they leave a class is a statement of what was important to know from the day's lesson.

Closure is the process of wrapping up a lesson with a student activity that reiterates what it is students need to know. Exit tickets or an exit journal can facilitate closure. The following are some examples of exit tickets:

- **ADVANCED ORGANIZER:** At the beginning of a third-grade class, give students an advanced organizer divided into four questions regarding what they know or think they know about Columbus coming to the New World (see format on page 28). For closure, revisit the advanced organizer and review whether the statements were true or false. Always follow up an advanced organizer by confirming the accuracy of the true/false statements; failure to do so could lock in the wrong answer for a student.

- **3, 2, 1:** After finishing the lesson, say to students, "Before you leave today, I'd like you to use the half-page I gave you to write three things that you learned today, two ways that what you learned can be used in the real world, and one question that you would like me to clarify tomorrow." This technique is easy to adapt for younger students. For example, following a lesson with second-grade students on geometric shapes, you can have them write down the names of three shapes, two places in the real world the shapes are used, and one question that can be used on a quiz.

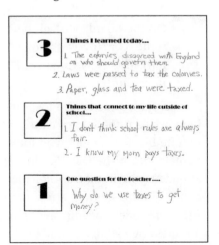

- **CIRCLE WEB:** Say to the class: "As your exit ticket, I'd like you to draw a circle in the middle of your paper and put six rays around the circle. In the middle I'd like you to write the name 'Thomas Jefferson.' On the rays, write six things that he is known for that we covered in class today."

Remember, a class shouldn't fizzle out. It should remain instructionally strong up to the exit bell. The teacher owns the last ten minutes! If students remember best what happens first and last, it's all the more reason to make the last few minutes of class count.

Let's do a final brief review of the four rules to powerful lesson design: identify targeted goals, activate prior knowledge, engage all learners, teach bell-to-bell. I've heard many a reference to the "art of teaching," and though I have seen some truly artistic educators, I know that teaching is not an art reserved for "talented" people, but a practice in which we all can excel if we choose to move forward on the journey to a brain-compatible classroom.

Reflection

1. In a subject or class that you taught recently, were components of brain-compatible lesson design evident? Discuss how you accomplished the following:

   - Adhered to the targeted learning goals
   - Activated students' prior knowledge to build connections to new content
   - Included strategies that engage and differentiate for learners
   - Provided closure

2. Using the lesson-design checklist on page 124, create a lesson that includes the important components of brain-compatible instruction. Remember to keep in mind the age-plus-or-minus-two-minute rule as well as the principle of M-capacity.

3. Consider the lesson you just designed. Take one aspect of the lesson and differentiate it for all students in your instructional group, classroom, or a hypothetical classroom.

4. **ACTIVATING PRIOR KNOWLEDGE (APK):** Reflect on strategies you used in high school and college classes to remember information for tests. In bulleted format, describe at least five such techniques.

Chapter 4

SAYING IT WITH PICTURES:
Improving Recall Using Nonverbal Memory Systems

OUR BRAINS REMEMBER pictures before words. This assertion shouldn't be news to most people. When we think that the written word is less than 10,000 years old—a very recent development in the history of mankind—it makes sense that pictures and images have a prominent place in our brain's ability to recall information.

Pictures have been used to enhance recall since early humans began communicating to one another which direction the next meal was heading! Locating the herd by using a map in the sand was likely a commonplace and effective approach to organizing the hunt. The caves of Lascaux in France, estimated to be 30,000 years old, contain amazing illustrations of Paleolithic man that convey events and stories of the period through distinct visual messages.

Pictures helped humans communicate long before written languages had been established.

We may not depend on images to survive in the same way early humans did millennia ago, but pictures remain a powerful way to communicate and activate memory. By extension, visual tools are a way for teachers to support students' learning and activate memory systems for learners of all ages.

Years back, I taught an introductory graduate-level course for teachers seeking certification in gifted education. I had recently learned a technique called *image-link*, which involves remembering text by associating pictures or images with the content in a connected, or linked, format. In a lesson using the work of Joe Renzulli, a prominent author and presenter in instruction for gifted students, I decided that an image-link would be a perfect way to help the class remember a key topic called "modifications of process"—in essence, ways teachers should adjust, or modify, instruction to best meet the needs of gifted learners. The five modifications of process I asked teachers to remember were freedom of choice, high-level thinking, open-endedness, discovery, and variety (Renzulli, 1986).

To help my students recall the information, I created an image-link (shown below). I explained to them that the flag represents *freedom of choice*. Then I elaborated, telling them that when choices are built into classroom instruction, students are more invested. Choices might mean anything from selecting the odd or even problems at the back of the chapter for homework to choosing a project topic or selecting partners in group work.

In this image-link, the mountains signify *high-level thinking*. Lessons that involve students in more complex thinking activate the brain more than passive, just-the-facts instruction. (We will expand on this topic in the next chapter.) The tunnel in the mountain stands for *open-endedness*. Too often, instruction in the classroom focuses on one right answer; yet, in our daily problem solving we try to consider as many possible solutions as we can, and pick the one we perceive to be the best. And when it comes to which television show to watch, snack to eat, or friend to call, students' thinking tends to be very open-ended!

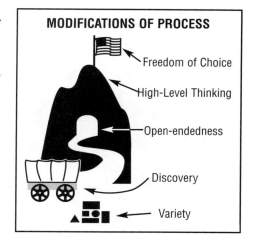

The pioneer wagon going west through the tunnel in the mountain represents *discovery*. When students discover something—a solution to a difficult problem, the true meaning of a tough concept, or insights into relationships between ideas or important people—there is that eureka moment tagged with emotion that boosts recall. Finally, *variety* is depicted in the goods and boxes that go in the pioneer wagon, which is going through the tunnel in the mountain with the flag on top (the link!). Presenting content in varied and novel ways will help students remember what has been taught. There is truth in the adage "Variety is the spice of life"!

When it came time to assess how my students had internalized these modifications of process, they demonstrated high success rates and declared that the image-link was the reason they could remember the concepts so readily.

I use this same illustration in workshops to show teachers the power of visual memory systems. First, I share the image-link and terms associated with the five modifications of process. Then I repeat the image-link connections two more times, without tipping my hand by overemphasizing the image connections. I know they will remember the pictures first—I just haven't told *them* yet because I want them to have a personal Aha! moment.

Then I proceed with the workshop.

Here's the clincher! At some point toward the end of a three-hour class or full-day workshop, I ask the participants to recall the five modifications of process as best they can, in writing. A few start to write, but most say something like, "I remember the pictures, but not the words. Can I draw the pictures?" Drawing the image helps the participants gain access to the word and its meaning. In fact, many individuals are able to retrieve the words rather quickly once they have sketched the images . . . but the pictures always come first, without fail!

Tapping Into the Visual Brain

Why do nonverbal strategies work? We know the occipital region is activated when images are being formed and that the primary visual cortex is the part of the brain that receives the earliest information from the eyes, by way of the thalamus (Sylwester, 2005). Research with people with verbal and visual impairments has revealed distinct nonverbal and verbal systems in the brain, further affirming that a nonverbal system in the brain exists (Smith, 2005).

Why do most of us have the ability to retrieve pictures before words? Consider a baby's developing brain. Incredible amounts of stimuli hit the visual cortex immediately after a baby is born. When our brain learns something new, synaptic connections are created; these connections increase significantly around the age of two to three months, peaking at about ten months (Blakemore & Frith, 2005). Think of it—as an infant absorbs her world through visual stimuli, neurons are hooking to other neurons, resulting in amazing synaptic growth during the first year of life. Indeed, a predisposition for using visual memory systems throughout life may be initiated at birth!

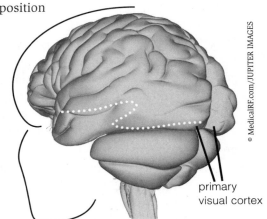

primary visual cortex

© MedicalRF.com/JUPITER IMAGES

The phrase "my mind's eye" may seem metaphorical, but it has great significance in light of brain-imaging techniques that provide insight to imagery-based learning and visual memory. Brain-imaging studies (Kosslyn, Ganis, & Thompson, 2001) reveal that, even with our eyes closed, simply imagining something stimulates about two-thirds of the same area in the brain that is activated when you actually view that thing. As you would expect, it is easier to retain concrete words—*beach*, *swim*, *palm trees*—than abstract words, such as *early*, *around*, *past*.

Each day, the visual cortex receives a flood of images by way of the eyes and the optic nerve.

Picture This!

Remember that amazing vacation? To experience how seeing in your mind's eye works, close your eyes, take a moment, and mentally return to a key location. Get a picture in your mind of the place, the scenery, faces of people who might have been present—and enjoy it for at least ten seconds. . . . What is happening? Your mind's eye is transporting you by activating most of the same neurons in the visual cortex that were activated when you were physically at the vacation site you remember so well.

VISUAL MEMORY HELPS US TAKE IN OUR WORLD

Visuospatial processing begins with the input of neural images in the visual cortex, which then proceed to the temporal lobe to be organized. What is of great interest is that visual memory is not limited to sensory data. In fact, limited sensory data cues are very much a part of our daily lives, and our visuospatial brain graciously compensates for partial information (Ratey, 2001). For example if we're driving down the highway and see the head of a dog out the window of a car, ears flying in the wind, we naturally assume that the rest of the dog is in the vehicle's back seat! We complete the picture. In a similar vein, if I am on the way to an evening event and am suddenly struck with the uncertainty of whether I turned off the oven, my mind visually retraces my steps in an attempt to recall whether the action occurred. Here are some other practical illustrations of visuospatial processing:

- When a friend asks directions to your house, you write down the directions or draw a map by envisioning the route from home to school.

- If you imagine mentally unloading your dishwasher and putting everything in its proper place, the entire kitchen is already *mapped* out in your brain as you mentally perform the task.

- Some people arrange their grocery list based on the first supermarket aisle they enter and the last aisle they leave. They picture the sequence and the position of items on the shelves as they write the list.

- When we clean out the closet and find an item from high school, the tangible artifact evokes visual images that take us back to the places, faces, and events of earlier life.

Quite simply, we depend on visual memory to negotiate the world around us. Once a picture of a location comes into the brain, additional related information appears. For example, remembering where you were during an event or activity often evokes more details: "Oh, yes, I lost my sunglasses at the football game. We sat in the second tier, close to the steps." Suddenly, a vivid picture comes to mind, of the location in the stands, the path in and out of the stadium, the food vendors barking their drinks and fries, the jostling crowd, and the game won or lost. In retrieving information about where the sunglasses might have ended up, numerous other visual cues fill in the picture—making it more complete. This visual recall makes sense, since an important life skill is remembering how to get from one place to another by picturing details of the location, the people you were with, and what was going on. Just think, how would humans have survived over the centuries if they could not find their way to and from base camp?

So what does a lost pair of glasses at a football game have to do with helping students as learners? Teachers who design lessons that tap into students' nonverbal memory systems, using visual cues, will aid recall and enhance learning. Just as my brain helped me make a detailed map of all the places my sunglasses might be, students will be able to use nonlinguistic stimuli to access information more completely.

Consider this example: Jen Morris, a middle school librarian, used blue painter's tape on her library floor to outline a giant map (15 by 30 feet) of the United States, complete with major rivers and mountain ranges. With library tables moved to one side, Jen worked with groups of students to research and review key geography and historical events that were part of the curriculum. Students "walked" the Missouri River with the Lewis and Clark expedition and stood on sites of key Civil War battles; they "traveled" to Mount Rushmore and the Grand Canyon. These strategies engaged students' visual memory systems and also included movement and emotional amplitude. When it came time to recall United States geography on a standardized test, the students were able to tap into these systems and remember the picture on the library floor. (The sensory-motor activity of walking the map assisted, as well!)

Curiously, most of us have a natural inclination to use visual prompts. Recently, I had a conversation with a teacher following a visit to her class. She taught part of her lesson from a whiteboard on the side of the room. Her work on the board had been erased, but as we discussed her lesson, I found myself pointing several times to the empty place where the content had been displayed—referring to the location where instruction had occurred.

Students do the same thing. Before administering a test, teachers often cover up instructional bulletin boards in the room and remove student projects from shelves or tables. Nevertheless, teachers tell me that when students get to specific questions, they gaze at the spaces on the walls or tables where the items used to be—as if visually reconstructing what had been there. If we make students aware that nonverbal techniques enhance recall, we can help them learn how to consciously activate these systems.

Visual Study Strategy

Our brain prompts our visual memory system to assist in recall, so we must strive to be more deliberate about helping students access this tool. Tell students that they will be able to "see" behind covered bulletin boards. Practice by telling them to close their eyes and remember as much of the picture or display as they can, then write or draw what they can recall on scratch paper, without looking. Discuss the power of visual recall to help them see the importance of nonverbal strategies.

Spatial Memory of Shapes, Objects, Artifacts, and Props

Another area of visual memory relates to identifying the shapes of objects and manipulating them in space. Many preschool and kindergarten activities involve such visual memory tasks as building, selecting alike shapes, and categorizing shapes based on attributes. Recall is encouraged by the visuospatial nature of the tasks, the place in the room where the activity occurs, and the kinesthetic component of students being physically engaged.

Artifacts are important nonverbal tools. In "Integrating the Curriculum" Heidi Hayes Jacobs speaks about having an artifact box in the room a few weeks prior to beginning a new unit of study (1992). These artifacts may include anything related to the topic. For a unit on seasons, children might bring in different kinds of leaves, a winter scarf, flip-flops, seeds, harvest gourds, or seasonal ornaments—all visual symbols that can be associated with seasons of the year. As students sort through the artifact box, they are pondering, trying to make connections: *What do flip-flops have to do with seasons? Oh, yes, you wear flip-flops in the summer because the weather is warm.* The artifacts are visual prompts that prime the brain. Although they will not start the unit for two to three weeks, students are already beginning to reflect on the content, priming the brain, which, in turn, builds readiness for the new information.

As a prompt for visual memory, artifacts are effective for tapping prior knowledge and

Artifacts Make Learning Strategies Concrete and Accessible

Third-grade teacher Laura Dewald created a Reading-and-Thinking Toolbox that uses artifacts as symbols for key reading comprehension strategies her students must remember and use. Here is her story:

> In my third-grade classroom, I use Mary Peterson's Reading-and-Thinking Toolbox to make reading comprehension strategies more accessible to my young readers. Peterson first introduced me to the idea at a workshop on reciprocal teaching. Students use the metacognitive reading strategies of *predict*, *question*, *clarify*, and *summarize* to gain a deeper understanding of the text. While the strategies are effective, my third-grade students often struggle with the terminology. Peterson suggests pairing each strategy with a concrete object, such as in the following examples:
>
>
> - Predict—a crystal ball (or clear snow globe)
>
> - Question—an interview microphone
>
> - Clarify—a magnifying glass
>
> - Summarize—a cell phone

helping students connect the new to the known; they are equally effective in creating images that reinforce specific facts, concepts, and strategies, as illustrated in the box above and the photograph on page 54. The photograph shows an old suitcase filled with artifacts that represent the ways railroad travel significantly changed the nation's economy after the Civil War. The contents include the following:

- An old map: symbolizing travel and moving from one place to the next, with references to specific cities and geographic features

- Fake money: representing people's need to make money to recover from the devastation of the war and the use of the railroad as a cheap, easy way to distribute goods

• Connect (a term I added)—a large jigsaw puzzle piece

Early in the school year, I have students share their background knowledge on the function of each tool, then I introduce the accompanying strategy name. I explain how the props are symbols. For example, when students use the microphone to question, they are prompted to think of interviews or talk shows that they have seen where a host asks questions into a microphone. When using the cell phone to summarize, I remind them that because it costs money to talk on a cell phone, they must save time and convey only the most important ideas from what they have read. I model, and we practice using the tools in shared and guided reading.

My students have become very familiar with applying the reading-and-thinking tools and using them throughout my classroom. Students use them independently at literacy centers. In the reading response center, students can complete graphic organizers that feature the image of each tool they used in their reading; in the library center, students can buddy-read and use a smaller toolbox with a buddy to help them better understand as they read. The toolbox is even useful in social studies and science as an additional support in making meaning from interactive note pages. The Reading-and-Thinking Toolbox has made reading comprehension strategies meaningful and even enjoyable for the students in my class.

• Postcards: indicating key cities that were connected by railroad

• Clothing and fabric: reflecting the textile mills that were built up around the state

• Lumber (wood): symbolizing the furniture factories that used railroads to ship goods

• Coal: indicating the rise of coal mines and use of coal to fire engines and produce energy

• Livestock: showing that farmers raised livestock for more than just family consumption once railroads could move animals and goods more efficiently

• Tobacco: depicting this huge industry that was revitalized when shipment by rail became possible

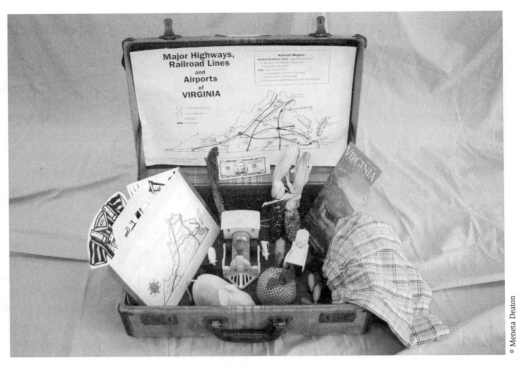

Using artifacts to remember the impact of railroads

Museum visits and field trips also facilitate recall on the part of students because of the artifacts and images. When I was an elementary school principal, our teachers attended a workshop where the presenter declared that field trips as culminating events were a backward strategy. Field trips should be taken before the unit of study, the speaker declared, so students would have mental pictures and images to which they could hook the content once they were back in the classroom, reading the printed materials that accompanied the unit (Kovalik & Olsen, 1997). A teacher I know took her second/third-grade combined class to visit the marine science museum prior to teaching her oceanography unit. A few days into the unit, she came to me saying, "I've taught this unit before, but never have I had students make so many connections. They seem to be carrying pictures of what they saw at the museum. I'm sold on doing field trips first!"

Additionally, props help students remember content and stay tuned in to the lesson. The first-grade teacher who dons the green Statue of Liberty crown before discussing the significance of this important national symbol will be able to tease her students into attentiveness with this prop. The Camp Fraction unit shared in Chapter 3 is another example of encouraging participation with novel items.

Visual Learning Tools for Gathering and Retrieving Information

Even without understanding the research on the brain's visual memory systems, teachers frequently use strategies that employ nonverbal cues. Before she learned about brain-compatible teaching, second-grade teacher Charla Curtis developed the following table, which requires students to activate both visual and verbal memory systems, simply because she thought it would help her elementary students understand new vocabulary. As new words are added, students create their own lexicons that include an image-prompt to aid recall. Other teachers have used visual modalities for many years because, through instructional practice, they know it works. Graphic organizers and image-enhanced note taking are two tools students usually find very helpful.

Name _____					
FINDING NEW WORDS					
WORD	DEFINE IT	DRAW IT	GIVE EXAMPLES	COMPARE IT	HOW WILL YOU USE IT
edible	Can eat			like: food NOT like: dirt	When I think about what to eat.
				like: NOT like:	

Graphic Organizers

I have had many conversations with teachers about how to effectively use graphic organizers to reflect content to be learned. Occasionally, teachers shrug them off as a bandwagon strategy that will go away soon enough. However, most teachers recognize these thinking maps as valid tools that should be included in good lesson design. Let's see how they help increase retention of information.

Can you remember as a student when you were sitting in a class taking a test and an answer wouldn't come to you? Did you ever find yourself trying to picture the text you studied the night before—hoping that it would trigger a memory? I've done it. Years ago as an undergraduate, I sat in the third row of an 8 a.m. sociology class, taking a major test. As I pondered a question that I just couldn't answer, I mentally kicked myself, telling myself that I *knew* the response to the question that was in front of me. Then I half-closed my eyes—as if I could look into the back of my brain—and told myself, "You studied it last night. It was on the right-hand side of the page, there was a graph above it and a heading *opposite.*" Whenever I share this story, teachers in the room always nod, "Yes, I've had the same experience."

What was happening? Since I was unable to retrieve the answer to the question through verbal memory systems, my brain was constructing a graphic organizer out of the pages of my sociology text and attempting to help me find the hoped-for response by telling me where on the page I had seen it the evening before. Students react the same way. A student who completes a four-square graphic organizer on ancient China (shown at right) and then finds a question about Chinese inventions on a quiz is likely to first access the information through his visual memory system, thinking, "I remember the picture. Inventions were in the bottom right-hand box of the four-square organizer. There was a picture of paper and a seismograph." The power of graphic organizers is that they tap into both verbal and visual memory systems.

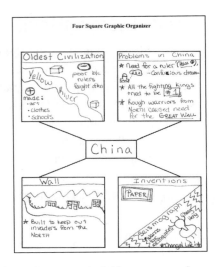

Graphic organizers are as varied and diverse as the teachers who use them; however, when selecting an organizer it is important to be clear about the thinking strategy that will be required of the student. For example, a student may use a Venn or multi-Venn diagram, or determine likenesses and differences using a compare/contrast thinking map. A sequence organizer is appropriate for rendering certain kinds of content, such as actions that led to the civil rights movement or the growth of a bean plant from seed to produce. Specific graphic organizers, including jellyfish, four-square, and T-charts, help students categorize or classify information. The chart on pages 57 and 58 helps you connect thinking strategies with organizer formats. Many reproducible versions of these organizers can be found online at sites such as www.graphic.org and www.eduplace.com/graphicorganizer.

Thinking Maps—A Systematic Approach

Teachers are free to devise their own graphic organizers or use structured systems of organizers that educators have created. Thinking maps (Hyerle, 1996) consist of eight graphic images associated with specific thinking skills. Schools that use these tools make an effort to have every teacher in the school employ the same eight thinking maps. The consistent application of these procedures encourages students to follow them when a thinking task is given.

Connecting Thinking Strategies and Graphic Organizers

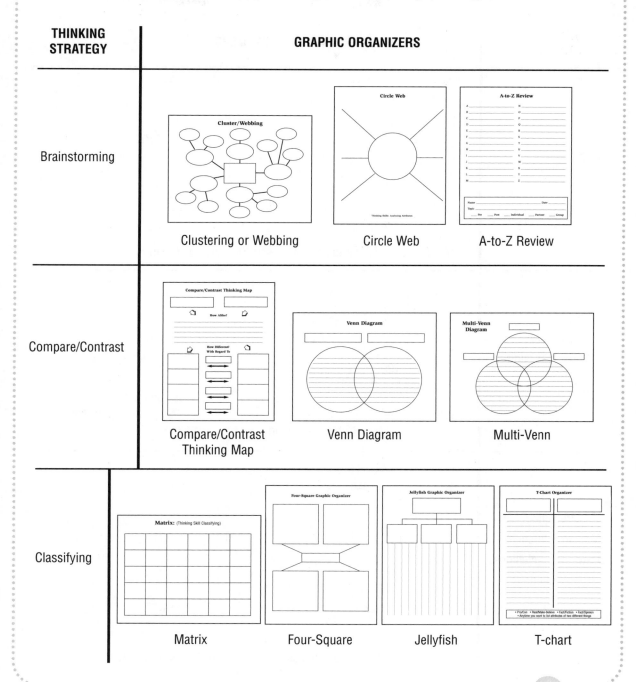

THINKING STRATEGY	GRAPHIC ORGANIZERS		
Brainstorming	Clustering or Webbing	Circle Web	A-to-Z Review
Compare/Contrast	Compare/Contrast Thinking Map	Venn Diagram	Multi-Venn
Classifying	Matrix	Four-Square	Jellyfish / T-chart

Connecting Thinking Strategies and Graphic Organizers

THINKING STRATEGY	GRAPHIC ORGANIZERS
Sequencing, Organizing	Sequence Character-Event *Also: Four-Square and Jellyfish—see "Classifying" organizers.
Visualizing, Problem Solving	Problem/Solution *Also: Character-Event— see "Sequencing, Organizing" organizers.
Predicting, Making Inferences, Drawing Conclusions, Evaluating	Reasons and Conclusions Plus-Minus Issue Organizer

IMAGE-ENHANCED NOTE TAKING

Teachers frequently tell me that students and taking notes don't mix. Begging, cajoling, coercing, and enticing students to take notes often frustrates teachers. But when we add a visual component, note taking becomes a useful, valued tool for both teachers and students. The point in this discussion is not to elaborate on particular styles of note taking, but rather, to present a case for including nonverbal representations as part of a note-taking system.

Split-page note taking is a version of taking notes in which the teacher asks the students to record content notes on the left two-thirds of the page while reserving the right third of each page for pictures or images related to the content. These pictures become mnemonics that will aid in recall of the content. Similarly, study guides developed by teachers should have a portion of the page left blank so students have space to draw image-links (see page 47) to help them remember the lesson or unit of study.

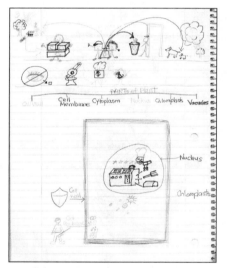 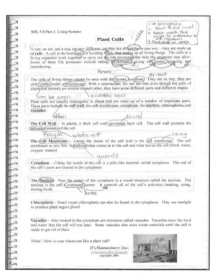

Interactive note taking in science includes APK with pictures (left) and vocabulary connections (right).

Interactive note taking is another system that uses pictures and images to help in the recall of content. I first encountered interactive note taking in a History Alive! workshop and have observed successful applications in history classrooms at all grade levels. Teachers subject areas have reported many positive responses from students about completing interactive notebooks. Interactive note taking has many iterations, but all involve visual and verbal memory systems working together to aid students in recalling information that has been taught.

Visually Based Learning Games

When learning is embedded in games, teachers get a twofer: targeted learning *and* student engagement. Games typically reinforce both verbal and non-verbal memory pathways but some games specifically activate the nonverbal memory system, using pictures, images, and/or artifacts.

PICTURE IT!

In Picture It! players compete to sketch the most recognizable image or picture cues for a given word. In a science lesson designed to reinforce weather-related terminology, the terms might include *clouds*, *precipitation*, *condensation*, and *humidity*. Though these are challenging words to draw, students usually come up with great visuals!

To conduct a classroom Picture It! task, have students work in pairs—partner A and partner B. Explain that they will be given a word in a PowerPoint slide, on the whiteboard, or in a sentence strip chart. Only the person drawing the words, (in this case partner A) can look at the word—partner B looks down at the paper or has his or her back to the word. (Curiously, the honor system has worked very successfully in all levels of classes.) Then partner A must do his or her best to draw images that reflect the word so partner B can guess it. No oral or written cues can be provided—the image is the only clue for partner B, who offers answers until he or she guesses the word correctly. Tell students that they must talk to each other at a whisper level, so they don't give the word away to others. The partners switch back and forth, drawing for two to four cycles. While scoring systems can be determined by the teacher, the energy of the game is usually enough to satisfy students.

THE MATCHING GAME

Teachers often construct homemade versions of this visual memory game by pasting or drawing pairs of pictures or writing words on small cards. Students arrange the cards in rows and columns then turn over two cards in hope of making a match. The teacher decides the matching attribute—a match could be based on the same sight word, words that rhyme, words and their definitions, or words that have the same root word or ending consonant. When students have to recall the word or picture from a given card and locate it spatially on the desk when it is turned over, they are using nonverbal tools.

Pointers for Infusing Visual Learning in Lesson Design

If capitalizing on the visual memory systems is beneficial to the learner, why don't we use them more extensively in instruction? Using nonverbal representations has been established as an effective instructional technique (Marzano et al., 2001), however, in many classrooms such representations are used sparsely or randomly.

In a brain-compatible lesson, the teacher must first consider the learning targets for students and the content of the lesson to be taught, then decide where to include learning activities that capitalize on visual memory pathways in the lesson. As an example, the following assignments are appropriate for students studying the Lewis and Clark expedition:

- Using a map of the United States, trace the route of Lewis and Clark from St. Louis to the Pacific. Mark significant locations where the expedition members camped by drawing an arrow to the location and a box. In the box, draw a picture with a brief description that says something significant about the expedition at the stop you selected.

- Using information available from the Lewis and Clark journals, draw a picture of the boats to scale. Try to show how much space was utilized for cargo.

- Research Sacagawea. Create an outline of her role on the expedition and draw a three-panel triptych representing three of her contributions during the Lewis and Clark expedition.

- Lewis and Clark identified many birds and animals that had not yet been discovered east of the Mississippi River. Using journal excerpts from the expedition (from textbooks or on the Internet) and an online encyclopedia, create a journal of five of the birds and animals that Lewis and Clark found most interesting and do your best to re-create the drawings yourself. Include a label and brief description next to your drawing.

BEING INTENTIONAL

In brain-compatible lesson design it's not sufficient to simply select from five bulleted assignments that use pictures, images, and nonverbal tasks for students. Teachers need to know why these activities help their students learn the targeted content. We need to ask ourselves, "Are the assignments simply nice activities using colored pencils and construction paper or an intentional effort to tap into visual memory systems to build recall?"

Being intentional means a teacher needs to know how these tasks relate to the key content to be learned, how mastery of the tasks will be assessed, the amount of time allowed to complete the task, and the procedures to be followed. For each of the tasks above, students need a clear explanation of the learning goal in order to produce quality work. These assessment tools also encourage students to self-assess how they are progressing.

For the project researching Sacagawea's contributions to the Lewis and Clark journey above, a teacher might outline the following criteria (often called "look-fors"):

- The outline reflects Sacagawea's participation in at least six distinct stages of the journey, as discussed in class.

- The outline is legible, using a standard format.

- The three-panel triptych is in sequence, from left to right.

- The drawings reflect three or more major contributions of Sacagawea during the expedition.

- The drawing is done in pen and ink, colored pencils, or fine-point magic markers.

- The drawings can be clearly deciphered by all viewers.

- The triptych can be a standing presentation or a flat rendering.

A Word About Not Overdoing Visual Representations

Students benefit from the deliberate activation of their visual memory systems but teachers need to be careful not to overuse nonverbal tasks. Keep in mind that our brains like novelty. However, the more a technique is used to build declarative memory of facts and concepts, the less novel it becomes. Wonderful strategies can become ho-hum if done repeatedly. Avoiding visual clutter is also important. Although using nonverbal memory systems enhances recall, creating an environment that has an *excess* of visual stimuli can be counterproductive. Classrooms that are overdone with posters, pictures, and/or "stuff" on the walls can interrupt a learner's ability to focus. Similarly, learning posters that are too busy and have an excess of words and/or pictures should be avoided. Visual stimuli for learning must relate to specific learning goals, using pictures and/or images that the student understands.

Foremost, a teacher should also be able to explain to students the rationale upon which the use of nonverbal memory systems is based—specifically that "our brains remember pictures before words, and doing these kinds of projects will help your brains recall important information." The skilled teacher will know how to incorporate activities using nonverbal memory systems into a *smarter* lesson plan!

CHANGING ATTENTION STATES TO KEEP LEARNERS ENGAGED

In the previous chapter, we learned that our brain learns best when we use a focus/refocus approach. Using nonverbal representations is a great way to help learners refocus from one attention state to another; teachers need to plan a portion of the lesson for the appropriate amount of time (remember the age-plus-or-minus-two-minutes guideline in Chapter 3), then shift focus by changing the mode of delivery. An example would be moving from a reading/questioning verbal activity—such as a guided-reading lesson—to one that activates the visual memory systems, such as using a plus-minus issue graphic organizer to depict an aspect of reading. These instructional shifts indirectly accommodate learning styles and/or multiple intelligences of students, as well.

When teachers are asked to create lessons using nonverbal representations, it is important to understand that these brain-compatible instructional strategies succeed because of the role of the visual cortex in memory. When used purposefully, strategies that incorporate images, pictures, artifacts, and props can become part of powerful lesson design.

Reflection

1. Think about a lesson you are about to teach. Develop three to four activities that tap into nonverbal memory systems that support the learning goal. Share these with a colleague.

2. Reflect on six to ten assignments or projects that you have given to your students. Create a table similar to the one below and list those assignments as best you remember. Now, identify the kind of assignment each one was. Select from the following five options:

   a) Mostly verbal (encoding)—speaking or writing

   b) Mostly verbal (decoding)—listening or reading

   c) Mostly verbal and numerical—computation/problem solving

d) Mostly visual (any strategy from this chapter)

e) Other (not verbal, visual, or numerical; e.g., kinesthetic)

Assignment	Learning System
Colonial Life Newspaper	b, d

Did the assignments reflect a balance between verbal (a, b, and c) and nonverbal (d and e) memory systems? Could you have adapted any of the assignments to help students capitalize on the brain's ability to recall pictures before words?

3. Consider graphic organizers an instructional tool and be deliberate about including several in your week's lessons. (See pages 56–58 for organizer formats and Web sources for printable organizers.) As you build a portfolio of these tools, consider the thinking strategies each targets and how it enhances the learning experience for students.

4. **ACTIVATING PRIOR KNOWLEDGE (APK):** "Students must do the work of thinking—teachers can't just tell them what they need to know" is an assertion made by many educators. What significance does this phrase have for teachers as they plan for students in their classes? How do you (or should you) get students to think?

Chapter 5

HIGHER-ORDER THINKING:
Make Students Do the Work!

SEVERAL YEARS AGO, I worked with a class of fifth graders as a guest teacher. I carried into the room a large box containing a soccer ball, basketball, football, baseball, volleyball, and golf ball and set it on the table. With little preface to the lesson, I showed the class the contents of the box and then asked for a volunteer to "come up and please pick out the right ball." A few students had raised their hands as soon as I asked for a volunteer, but then, looking a bit perturbed, pulled them back down when they heard me say "the right ball."

One student still had her hand up. I asked, "Do you want to come up and pick out the right ball?" She responded, "You didn't give us enough information to know which ball is the right ball." A number of students agreed. "Oh," I said with surprise, "What other information do you need?" They explained that they needed to know what game was being played or if the ball was being bounced, kicked, or hit. Others mentioned they might need to know if the ball was big or little. I asked them to listen to additional phrases and tell me which ball came to mind: *pitch* the ball, *serve* the ball, *hike* the ball, *putt* the ball, *head* the ball, *sink* the ball. They agreed that with each phrase, a clearer picture of the "right" ball came to mind.

Next, I asked them to select "the best ball" and write three reasons supporting their choice on the scratch paper provided. As they wrote, I noted that students' responses seemed more confident than with the first request, since *best* is a subjective term. I then put each ball in a different spot around the room and asked class members to go to the one they selected. Students then shared their perspectives with one or two other classmates on why this ball was the *best* ball.

I used this anticipatory set to help students examine words in context and detect key phrases that communicate the purpose, perspective, or intent of a text. My conversation with students was an effort to encourage thinking and avoid the "telling the information quickly so we can move on" syndrome.

Planning for a Thinking Classroom

Even with the best of intentions for building higher-order thinking into instruction, I would not have been able to carry off this lesson on the spot, without preplanning. The lesson worked because I had designed in advance the conditions to disarm students and provoke them to think. In short, I deliberately developed a lesson where students used their brains!

In this chapter we will be discussing strategies to activate higher-order thinking—some new, some familiar—with a focus on being intentional about infusing critical and creative reflection into instruction on a daily and weekly basis. A second emphasis will be to ask you to analyze who is doing the *work* of thinking in your classroom. (If the teacher is doing all the brainwork, it's the teacher who will grow synapses—not the students.)

BEGINNING WITH METACOGNITION

Knowing *how you know* is a foundation strategy of thinking. Referred to as metacognition, this "knowing" includes awareness of one's own activities while reading, processing information, and studying, accompanied by self-regulation on the part of the learner (Brown, 1988). When students become conscious of their thinking, they are able to be more deliberate about applying different comprehension and/or problem-solving strategies.

The fifth graders were so eager to respond to my first question that they enthusiastically raised hands when they heard my initial phrase, "I need a volunteer . . ." Their first thought was "I'm confident about raising my hand for just about anything, so let's go!" As soon as I completed the sentence, ". . . to pick out the *right* ball," students began to self-regulate their thinking. The metacognitive process students used throughout my lesson about the *right* and *best* ball to select likely included the following key elements of reasoning.

Thinking Element	Student's Self-Talk About Thinking
Identification of Purpose	The teacher's question is vague. I can only find the *right* ball with additional information.
Prior Knowledge	Based on what I know about playing games using different kinds of balls, I believe I can identify the specific ball if I receive more information, such as an action verb.
Perspective	I've played and watched many games and have an opinion about which one I think is the best.
Supportive Evidence	I can provide three reasons to support why I think a specific ball is best.
Interpretation or Conclusions	Sharing with other students, I gained additional insight and support for my conclusion as to why a ball was the best.

BUILDING THINKERS OR TEST TAKERS?

Thinking about thinking has both challenged and entertained philosophers and scientists over the ages. Teachers are not strangers to this idea of metacognition; primary and elementary teachers often use the term "think-alouds" to describe the commonly used approach of talking students through the process of how they might self-regulate thinking about a question, topic, or prompt.

Educators have always focused on thinking, so we might conclude that they have figured out the perfect system for producing thinkers. After all, isn't producing thinking citizens a key component of every school system's mission statement? Don't we assess students extensively to measure how well they think? (So you detect a bit of cynicism.)

We all know that mandatory standards assessments do not result in developing thinkers. In fact, there is evidence that strict adherence to teaching to the test impedes higher-order thinking (Darling-Hammond, 1997). Results of standardized tests in grades 3 through 12 in Virginia school systems revealed that the questions most frequently missed by students were identified as higher-order questions involving complex thinking (Mulligan, 2007).

With so many facts that students must know for "the test," teachers often default to teacher-talk to convey content—telling students what they need to know to make sure everything has been taught. In such situations, students' developing as thinkers is a hoped-for by-product and, at worst, an incidental occurrence.

In some remarkable classrooms, higher-order thinking is consistently cultivated, but significant work needs to be done to make *every* classroom one where reflection and reasoning are nurtured—where students truly do the work of thinking. To be successful in this endeavor, teachers most both prepare students for "the test" *and* teach them to be creative and critical thinkers. The two efforts are not mutually exclusive and are attainable if we are intentional about designing instruction to encourage thinking.

DEVELOPING THINKING: IS IT EVER TOO LATE?

When I've discussed higher-order thinking in workshops, teachers have asked, "What if the teachers before me haven't emphasized high-level thinking? Is it too late for students to start now?" The answer is a resounding "No!" We can develop and encourage thinking throughout the school years and beyond—so it is never too late to start. (Remember, synapses grow all our lives!) If every teacher resolved to foster critical and creative thinking from this day forward, think how much more successful—and engaged—our students would be.

Students benefit when we teachers enhance our own thinking, as well. A teacher's metacognitive self-monitoring related to encouraging students as thinkers is evident in the "I" questions discussed at the end of Chapter 1:

Do I construct lessons so *students* do the thinking?	• I design lessons that minimize teacher talk and maximize student thinking.
	• I design lessons so the students do the work.
	• I model through think-alouds.
	• When students respond, I ask them to support responses using the text.
	• I create questions that solicit higher-order thinking.
Do I consistently make connections to students' daily lives?	• I help students make personal connections to their lives to address the question "Why do I need this?"
	• In every lesson, I make sure my students see the relevance for today.

Taking the survey Building a Thinking Classroom (page 126) will help you assess how well your instruction supports students as *thinkers*. Use the survey to generate discussions among your grade-level team, learning community, or entire faculty about which indicators are most/least evident in your learners.

Higher-Order Thinking and the Brain

Just as passing a test does not guarantee that students exercise their thinking brains, *remembering* does not necessarily encompass higher-order thinking. In Chapter 2, we discussed the memory systems and the importance of designing instruction to help students move information from working memory to long-term memory to ensure recall of content. However, students can activate rote, automatic, and/or procedural memory systems with little or no involvement in high-level thinking. For example, let's say that students are asked to memorize the Great Lakes using the mnemonic HOMES. Getting the facts—Huron, Ontario, Michigan, Erie, Superior—is enhanced, but on Bloom's Taxonomy the task is still at Bloom's knowledge level. (See pages 71 and 72 for a list and brief description of Bloom's levels.)

THE THINKING BRAIN AT WORK

Although a diagram of the brain cannot be cleanly partitioned to show where reasoning and high-level thinking occur, specific areas do activate during these tasks. The prefrontal cortex (directly behind the forehead) coordinates and integrates most brain functions. Sometimes referred to as "the brain's CEO," the prefrontal cortex handles the executive functions of decision making, planning, and problem solving. Additionally, the two frontal lobe pathways process foresight—rational, logical thought processes, as well as insight—social skills and empathy functions (Sylwester, 2005). The prefrontal cortex activates when students are challenged with higher-order thinking and problem-solving tasks.

Another area of the brain involved in reasoning is the cingulate gyrus, located on top of the corpus callosum, which connects the two hemispheres of the brain. If the prefrontal cortex is the brain's CEO, the cingulate gyrus is the executive assistant who sizes up incoming sensory information according to its emotional significance, determining whether it's benign or intense, and forwards the information to the prefrontal cortex for attention, decision, and action (Sylwester, 2005). Unlike the amygdala, which activates the fight, flight, or freeze automatic responses, the cingulate gyrus gets involved when the situation is less dire and there is time to coordinate retrieval of pertinent information that will assist in making an informed, and perhaps creative, decision. According to Sylwester, "The cingulate helps us to make up our mind consciously about what to do when we confront ambiguous problems with several possible solutions" (p. 46).

In Chapter 1, we discussed how the right hemisphere of the brain primarily processes novel challenges while the left hemisphere processes knowledge and effective routines that may have been used previously when confronted with similar challenges (Sylwester, 2005). When searching for a solution to a problem, it's as if our left brain says, "Why start from scratch? Let's see if we already have information in storage that will help out!" For example, a few years ago, when I was trying to remedy the results of a bee assault on my youngest son on the sidelines of a soccer field, I

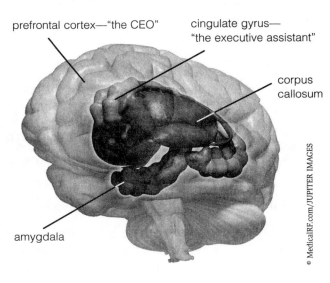

prefrontal cortex—"the CEO"

cingulate gyrus—"the executive assistant"

corpus callosum

amygdala

© MedicalRF.com/JUPITER IMAGES

Key decision-making areas of the brain

remembered that my mother had always treated my bee stings with a paste of baking soda and water (left-hemisphere recall). However, since I did not have baking soda, I innovated (a right-brain solution) by substituting toothpaste—a non-gel sample I had in my handbag—for baking soda. Despite my son's skepticism, I applied the white paste, which alleviated the sting.

What does this mean for the classroom? The brain seeks connections to what is already known, regardless of the novelty or familiarity of the stimulus. If a student is asked to solve a problem that is new or unfamiliar, his or her brain automatically looks through the lens of known experiences in order to solve the new problem. Thus, before the brain accepts a stimulus as novel or new, it quickly scans to see if existing experiences might assist.

HIGHER-ORDER-THINKING FRAMEWORKS

The fact that our brains are wired to use prior experiences to solve problems and filter new information tells us that our persistent effort to make sense out of the world around us is innate. Making sense—and finding meaning—is the foundation of higher-order thinking. The challenge for teachers is to capitalize on this meaning-making inclination by designing instruction that is relevant, interesting, and stimulating.

For starters, let's think about how we can be deliberate about designing lessons so students do more than search for the one right answer. In this regard, how we frame the question becomes critical. Here are examples of some open-ended questions that encourage student reflection:

- Is there a pattern?
- Why did this occur?
- What must change to avoid the same result?
- How can we learn from what happened?
- What steps are needed to accomplish the task?
- If these are the attributes, what is the category?
- How many solutions can you identify for the problem?
- If this is the answer, how many problems can you write to make it true?

If each teacher had to create his or her own hierarchy for questioning and thinking, our task would be even more challenging. Fortunately, a number of frameworks for thinking have been developed to support students' skills and to serve as guides to support thinking. In the rest of this chapter we'll look at several of these frameworks, beginning with Bloom's Taxonomy.

Bloom's Taxonomy

In 1976, Benjamin Bloom created a taxonomy that has influenced teacher training and classroom instruction for well over three decades. As a teacher in training, I had to memorize the six levels of the taxonomy and write lesson objectives according to each level. At that time, I shrugged off the taxonomy as rather confining. I thought writing objectives according to the six levels of Bloom was a bit much, and anyway, how could we be sure that a particular student was processing at a more complex level? As a new teacher, I agreed that my class should be engaged in high-level thinking tasks. I even made sure to give my students plenty of opportunities for critical and creative thinking, but these activities tended to be stand-alone brainteasers or one-shot activities that were not tied to the learning goals. I had a sincere intent—but a faulty plan.

Fast-forward to a decade later, and I reach for my copy of Bloom when I begin to work more actively with teachers on ways to infuse lesson plans with opportunities for thinking. This time, I see how the taxonomy works within a lesson and makes a clear distinction between higher-order and lower-order thinking. I tell teachers in workshops, "Relax— you've already mastered a third of the taxonomy without a second thought because the majority of questions and activities we give students are at Bloom's knowledge and comprehension levels." Then I explain that teachers have 50 percent of the taxonomy internalized if they consistently and effectively design tasks at the application level. However, I caution that a key for the application level is having students do something new or original with the content—a criterion that is not always understood.

I have provided the revised Bloom's Taxonomy (Anderson & Krathwold, 2000) on page 72. The new Bloom's Taxonomy category headings are more active. For example, *synthesis* is changed to *creating*. Additionally, the order of the taxonomy has shifted slightly to place synthesis/creating at the top of the hierarchy, after evaluation, and descriptions of the taxonomy are accompanied by action-focused prompts.

	ORIGINAL TAXONOMY	**REVISED TAXONOMY**
Higher-Order	Evaluation	Creating
	Synthesis	Evaluating
	Analysis	Analyzing
Lower-Order	Application	Applying
	Comprehension	Understanding
	Knowledge	Remembering

	TAXONOMY	VERBS	
HIGHER-ORDER THINKING	**Synthesis/Creating** Putting together ideas or elements to develop an original idea or engage in creative thinking	Design Construct Plan Experiment Create	Produce Invent Devise Synthesize
	Evaluation/Evaluating Judging the value of ideas, materials, and methods by developing and applying standards and criteria	Check Hypothesize Critique Evaluate	Judge Test Detect Monitor
	Analysis/Analyzing Breaking information down into its component elements	Compare/Contrast Organize Deconstruct Arrange	Attribute Outline Structure Integrate
LOWER-ORDER THINKING	**Application/Applying** Using strategies, concepts, principles and theories in new situations	Implement Carry out Use Execute	Convey Model Depict Illustrate
	Comprehension/Understanding Understanding of given information	Interpret Summarize Classify Support	Retell Infer Paraphrase Explain
	Knowledge/Remembering Recall or recognition of specific information	Recognize List Describe Identify	Retrieve Name Locate Find

Here are some examples of how an upper-grade literature response assignment might be designed at each level of Bloom's Taxonomy. The prompts have been developed for *The Fighting Ground* by Avi (Harper & Row, 1987).

KNOWLEDGE: Identify five encounters Jonathan had during his 24 hours away from home.

COMPREHENSION: What distinguished the Hessians from the British and why were they feared?

APPLICATION: Use a character/event graphic organizer and describe how Jonathan's emotions changed at four different points between 9:58 and 3:16. In each trait area, write a word that describes his emotion related to the event you selected.

ANALYSIS: Find three situations that show different ways the corporal interacts with Jonathan over the day. How do his actions compare to those of soldiers today?

EVALUATION: War and conflict persist in our world. In your opinion, can young people today influence the outcome of war? Provide reasons for your response.

SYNTHESIS: As Jonathan comes home at 10:30 the next morning, he hears his dad hoeing in the field—a sound that "filled him, pushing away the pain." From Jonathan's perspective, write a poem, letter to a family member, story, or newspaper editorial that expresses his pain.

MOVING TOWARD SYNTHESIS

It is much more common for teachers to give lower-order thinking prompts than to challenge their students with higher-order thinking questions or tasks at the levels of analysis, evaluation, or synthesis. Of the three higher levels, most teachers seem comfortable assigning tasks at the levels of analysis and evaluation, such as:

- "What effect would eliminating the step of evaporation have on the water cycle?"

- "Select a position for or against the seriousness of global warming and justify your opinion."

Synthesis is the most complex level of Bloom's Taxonomy. To better understand what synthesis encompasses, imagine a funnel. The wide end of the funnel suggests that to synthesize or create, a learner must consider all the information he or she has acquired on

Synthesis Activity: One Decision, Big Changes

Directions: Consider the characters in the book _____. Select a key character and change a decision or action that particular character made in the story. Rewrite or visually depict what might occur in the whole story or just a section, based on the change you made. When you submit the product, include at least five "look-fors" that will guide my review of your work.

SAMPLE LOOK-FORS

1. I selected a key character important to the story.

2. I selected a flip chart 3-D organizer for a combined visual and written description.

3. The first flip page tells the change I made and the other sections tell what happens because of this change.

4. I identified how my character responded with each event I wrote about.

5. I used words and pictures to tell about the events.

6. My work was neat and easy for the teacher to understand.

7. I used color and drew visual cues to elaborate.

---

a given subject—all of it must be poured into the funnel. Synthesis means taking in all that information, then consolidating it, compacting what's extraneous, and summarizing the contents in a succinct, specific manner—a process of narrowing down, depicted by the narrow, focused end of the funnel.

When planning a lesson, take into consideration that synthesis activities are open-ended and often take more time—particularly if a physical product is involved. Also, these tasks are more effective if students help establish criteria for their work, such as in the student task and look-fors above.

This synthesis activity asks students to change one element of a story and then re-create the scene or scenes that follow, showing the impact of this one change on the development of the story. Keep in mind that prerequisites for this assignment include giving students practice in establishing criteria for their work and presenting strong and weak products of this specific activity so students have a frame of reference for their end product. (Teachers may need to co-write the criteria with students, depending on students' ages and skill levels.)

When students help define the standards for their work—using criteria lists, "look-fors," or rubrics—they also are being asked to think critically about the task at hand. Additionally, when a student attempts to hand in a marginal product, we don't have to simply accept a grade; we can hand it back and put the assessment responsibility on the student by saying: "I'm worried that this isn't your best work. Before I accept it, I want you to go to the look-for list and see if you have met all the targets. Bring back your work and share with me areas you think could be improved." A student's ability to critique his or her own work includes self-regulation of thought—an important aspect of higher-order thinking.

SYNTHESIS ACTIVITIES

Strategies that help students synthesize or summarize content should be part of every teacher's repertoire. Teachers who merely encourage students to "put the story in your own words" or "tell it another way" often find that students consistently struggle to summarize essential information. In their lessons, teachers need to model the thinking processes and introduce structures that help students break up the process into manageable parts. The following activities provide this structure and are especially helpful.

CINQUAIN: A novel way to have students summarize or synthesize their thoughts on a concept or topic is to have them write a cinquain about it. The cinquain is a simple five-line poem that encourages students to reflect on the meaning of an idea or information just learned, and provides opportunities for creative expression.

Guidelines
Line 1: Write a one-word title (usually a noun).
Line 2: Describe the topic in two words (usually two adjectives).
Line 3: Show several actions associated with the topic, in three words (usually three "-ing" words).
Line 4: Express a feeling in a four-word phrase about the topic.
Line 5: Write a one-word synonym that restates the essence of the topic.

Examples

Reading	Equation	Photosynthesis
Words, stories	Always balances	Light, energy
Thinking, sharing, learning	Solving, equaling, operating	Transporting, tubing, turning
Traveling in our minds	Both sides treated fairly	Carbon dioxide into sugars
Books	Solution	Chlorophyll

SOMEBODY WANTED BUT SO: This construct provides a format for students to summarize information (Macon, Bewell, & Vogt, 1991). A significant amount of content can be summarized by identifying a main character or actor, the key problem, the conflict that results, and the outcome.

Somebody (Character)	Wanted (Key Problem)	But (Conflict)	So (Outcome)
Charlotte wanted to do something to save Wilbur's life, *but* she didn't know how to help *so* she tried spinning words into her spiderwebs to make people believe he was a very special pig.			
Lewis and Clark wanted to discover a navigable water route from the Mississippi to the Pacific Ocean *but* they were unsuccessful *so* they traveled by foot and boat to the Pacific and a year later returned home with maps and scientific journals of their trip.			

DISCARDING A MYTH

Bloom's Taxonomy is a framework for thinking, not a hierarchy. Students do not have to master the lower levels of the taxonomy *before* moving to higher levels. In fact, the levels are often used in combination. Clearly, lower-level facts must be used in higher-order thinking, and higher-order concepts often help cement knowledge-level facts into memory.

But when teachers default to lower-level questions and activities—particularly for lower-achieving students—they unintentionally limit them. The idea that struggling learners need consistent higher-order reflection is not a typical mind-set of educators. Teachers have said to me, "I work on higher-level thinking in the classroom, but Johnny isn't ready for it yet." I admit that I have said and have heard teachers say, "I have these enrichment activities for the students who finish their work early." Or even, "I differentiate by developing higher-level questions for students in the top group." What about nurturing higher-order thinking in struggling learners? Frankly, this area is one where I would welcome a "do-over" opportunity for my early years of teaching.

So let's rethink this! If synapses grow the more student's brains are activated, why would we deprive at-risk students of the very thinking tasks that will help them make more connections? Whether Bloom's or other frameworks are used, we must give students chances to work at higher-order thinking tasks at the youngest age possible in order to build their brainpower. Too often we have a mind-set that at-risk students need practice in the basics before moving to higher-order thinking. The opposite is true. The comprehension skills of classifying, sequencing, comparing/contrasting, drawing conclusions, and cause and effect—just to name a few—all exercise the brain. All learners deserve the opportunity to grow as thinkers—and the earlier we begin, the better!

High-Level Thinking Tasks Benefit <u>All</u> Students

When I was a principal, I learned a wonderful lesson about not underestimating the thinking abilities of at-risk students. In my school, an enrichment teacher was assigned to work with gifted students at all grade levels. As part of early identification of gifted students, she would teach whole-class lessons to kindergartners, emphasizing divergent, creative thinking so she could identify students who were potentially gifted.

One day, she came to my office after a particular lesson, and she was quite excited. "I have to tell you what just happened!" she said. "I was doing a lesson on creative thinking and you'll never guess who was amazing." I looked at her expectantly. "Shakee!" Now, I did look surprised, because this child was considered severely at-risk. He was sent to the office frequently for being unmanageable in the classroom. His language skills were more typical of a 4-year-old. Shakee definitely didn't seem to be anywhere near "gifted."

The enrichment teacher explained that she had been doing divergent, open-ended thinking activities, such as: Imagine this yardstick was something else—what could it be? Think of as many things as possible that have triangles. What would happen if there was winter year-round? One of the keys to Shakee's success was that these questions were open-ended and did not have one right answer. When he realized there were no wrong answers and he wasn't going to be judged for an incorrect response, he just blossomed. According to the enrichment teacher, "Shakee's input was more free-flowing and creative than the responses from the prospective gifted kids that had been referred by teachers for early identification." The story swept the school and several teachers who worked with Shakee saw him through a new lens.

The dilemma is that teachers can't just plop a higher-order question in the laps of all learners and expect for them to supply a creative answer. Some students walk into school more prepared for higher-order thinking than others, but all students can build these skills. Obviously, when assigning more complex tasks—at all levels—teachers should move from the familiar to the unfamiliar to scaffold thinking.

For example, if I am working with second graders to develop skills in cause and effect, I might begin with straightforward examples: Running in the hall will result in what? Not bringing in your homework on time will result in what? Eating too many marshmallows will result in what? After developing the concept of if/then or cause and effect you can introduce more challenging examples: "The weather forecaster said there was a 95 percent chance of rain today, but Lettie ran out of the house with only her book bag for the two-block walk to the bus stop. What might happen?"

With sufficient modeling, students can then work with partners to devise their own cause-and-effect "puzzles" to try and stump each other and the teacher. The idea of course is to increase complexity while still reinforcing the comprehension strategy of cause and effect.

When talking with teachers about ways to build in higher-order thinking on a consistent basis, I advise them to write down the powerful questions ahead of time. Teachers rarely deliver a compelling higher-order question spontaneously. Questions and higher-level activities need to be crafted ahead of time to ensure that students are challenged and remain focused on targeted learning goals.

DEVELOPING DIVERGENT THINKERS

Questions and tasks that foster open-ended thinking can free students from the "I only need to know the right answer" mind-set. Middle school teachers who work with the highest-achieving students have told me many times their most accelerated students have tepid responses to open-ended activities. These learners seem to want the efficiency of memorizing the right answer for the test on Friday. I worry that high achievers will miss key skills of critical and creative thinking because of a "just the facts" mentality that is reinforced by standards testing and the pressure of "getting the grade." However, as a guest teacher, I find that if I explain novel instructional strategies as techniques that will "grow synapses" and give students some background information about how the brain learns, they are quite receptive to a variety of instructional methods.

Practice in divergent, open-ended thinking assists in real-life problem solving as well. Creative thinking is evident when new and original ideas are produced. Another important framework, developed by Paul Torrance (1984), identifies four attributes of creative thinking:

FLUENCY: the ability to generate many ideas (*Think of all possible technology tools or devices that are used at home or school.*)

FLEXIBILITY: the ability to generate many different ideas (*Consider multiple uses of existing technologies or those that could be developed.*)

ORIGINALITY: the ability to generate unique ideas (*Reflect on new or novel technologies that might be developed over the next 50 years.*)

ELABORATION: the ability to generate many details (*Select one of the prospective technologies and provide additional details about its possible function and form.*)

It's "A Synapse Thing"

Teachers have come up to me after workshops saying, "I'm very excited about what I learned today, but I'm afraid my students won't be responsive if I try out new things." I explain that it is easier if the culture of brain-compatible instruction is established the minute students walk into the classroom at the beginning of the year or term; however, when teachers are ready to change their approach halfway through the year, I recommend telling the class, "I went to a workshop yesterday and I finally found out what my job is!" Of course, the students look skeptical, and someone typically says, "What do you mean what your job is? You're a teacher." The re-energized teacher's response should be, "My job is to help you grow synapses! From here on in, everything we do in class will be designed to help you grow synapses."

One teacher came back with this testimonial: "Now when I try something new, some students still roll their eyes, but they say in good humor, 'This is a synapse thing, isn't it?' I smile and respond, 'Absolutely!'"

Teaching students these attributes of creative thinking can provide a common language for the classroom. A physical science teacher can refer to a goal of developing *fluency* when asking students to think of as many uses for magnets at home and school as they can. Similarly, a fifth-grade social studies teacher could refer to *flexibility* or *originality* of thinking when asking students to think about all the options the founding fathers of our nation may have considered when forming a government, and what other alternatives might have been discussed.

Creative Thinking in Practice

Strategies to develop a student's ability to think creatively often serve as a basis for critical thinking that follows. Think tanks in the corporate or government sectors will often initiate sessions with statements such as "If money is not an option and no present boundaries exist, how could this problem be addressed most effectively?" or "Brainstorm every positive and negative result of this decision—regardless of how seemingly obscure the result might seem." Both tasks involve fluency and flexibility of thinking—with originality and elaboration as by-products. The quest for educators is to incorporate these techniques into lesson design while still making efficient use of time.

Another framework of divergent questions is suggested by educational consultant Roger Taylor. These open-ended questions foster creative thinking. Sample questions or tasks in the areas of quantity, viewpoint, forced association and reorganization encourage divergent thinking as seen in the chart below.

Some ideas for incorporating divergent questioning in lessons include:

- **Writing out your questions beforehand.** Do this for two reasons: (1) It takes a few minutes to think through what you want the question to be based on the content you are working with, and (2) if you think you will just do it when it "feels right," it will never get done. Divergent questioning is rarely spontaneous.

- **Focus on one questioning model at a time.** Pick a model each day or insert one kind of question per lesson—don't try to use all the types of questions at once. (Do give an initial introduction to the four questioning models with an explanation of why the models are helpful for sparking original ideas and how and when you will use them in class.)

- **Focus on viewpoint, forced association, and reorganization models.** Most teachers already do a good job with the quantity model (brainstorming).

- **Allow think time before accepting responses.** A good strategy is to use Think-Pair-Share to allow everyone to have some input before whole-group discussion.

Making Connections With Forced Association

Forced-association thinking tasks are categorized as *synectics* (Gordon, 1961). *Synectikos* is a Greek word referring to the fitting together of seemingly diverse elements in an effort to find relationships between what appear to be unrelated topics. Using metaphor and analogy, this construct taps into the brain's remarkable capacity to connect these seemingly unrelated elements and sparks surprising new ideas. Examples of synectic thinking include:

- **DIRECT ANALOGY:** How is a cafeteria like a beehive? Math like a schoolbus? Magnetism like middle school?

- **PERSONAL ANALOGY:** How does it feel to be a book in your classroom? What changes would you experience if you were condensation in the water cycle? How would you describe the school if you were a bird? A worm?

- **SYMBOLIC ANALOGY, COMPRESSED CONFLICT, OR OXYMORON:** When is silence deafening? Can painful goodness exist? What is comic tragedy?

The forced-association questions in the framework adapted from Taylor are often uncomfortable for teachers, yet students thrive on them. A number of years ago, I taught a

Divergent Questioning Model

In an effort to encourage unique and divergent thinking and to stimulate originality, the following questioning models can be utilized in all subject areas.

QUANTITY MODEL
Pattern:

How many ways . . . ?

List the reasons for . . .

List all of the . . .

Examples

- List as many words as you can that might go into a story about winter.
- List all the nonrenewable resources you can think of.
- How many things in your house can you think of that use magnets?

VIEWPOINT MODEL
Pattern

How would this look to a . . . ?

What would this look like to a . . . ?

What would _____ think about _____?

Examples

- How would a frog view a squirrel's habitat?
- What would a mail carrier's activities look like to an ant?
- You are the Mississippi River. What role have you had in settling North America?
- You are a triangle. Tell us how the Pythagorean theorem affects you.

FORCED ASSOCIATION MODEL
Pattern

How is a _____ like a _____?

How can you get ideas from _____ to help you work on _____?

Examples

- How is Martin Luther King, Jr., like an automobile?
- How is Huck Finn like tractor?
- How is writing a research paper like planting a garden?

REORGANIZATION MODEL
Pattern

What would happen if . . . ?

Suppose _____ occurred. What would be the consequences?

Examples

- What would happen if there were no tectonic movement in the earth?
- Suppose global warming caused countries along the equator to become more desertlike. What would be the consequences?
- What would happen if the Revolutionary War had been won by England?
- How would life be different if paper had never been invented?

series of workshops and gave the practicing teachers an assignment to use forced-association questions with students prior to the next session. Before leaving the class, one seasoned teacher shook her head and said, "I'll try them, but I don't like them!" While debriefing in the next class, she announced she was a changed woman. She declared, "I didn't like them, but my students loved them and asked for more of *those* questions all week." In her testimonial to the class, she highlighted one of the questions she had given her fourth-grade students: "How is Martin Luther King, Jr., like an automobile?" She then shared her student's insightful responses:

- An automobile takes you places and Martin Luther King took us places.

- An automobile has many colors, and he wanted everyone to accept each other even if they were of different colors.

- An automobile has an engine and he was like an engine to change discrimination.

During these forced association reflections, a student's brain retrieves everything it can about Martin Luther King, Jr., while almost simultaneously recalling all it can about cars. Picture a ladder. One structural side post is everything a student knows about Martin Luther King, Jr.; the other side is everything he or she recalls about automobiles. The rungs of the ladder are the connections between the two that his or her brain makes. When we ask students to hook two things together that seem unrelated, they dig deeper within their brains to find how the two things relate. There have been times when I have felt that I could actually see my students' thinking processes as they reflected on forced-association problems.

Committing to Fostering Divergent Thinking

Incorporating divergent thinking prompts in their lessons may feel awkward to some teachers. Some might see creative thinking tasks as frivolous or off task—which they potentially can be if they are not tied to the learning goals. However, since the learning brain pays attention to novel or new encounters, teachers may need to go beyond their own comfort zone in this regard in order to engage students and promote learning. These novel, out-of-the-box questions are just what some students need to be encouraged toward more fluent understanding and original thinking.

We also discussed in earlier chapters that our brains prefer to focus on information to be learned, then back off and apply the information before moving to additional or new content. Thus, in smart lesson design, teachers need to shift the focus of the lesson to keep students engaged. A well-constructed, creative question after a sustained mini-lecture, listening, or writing activity can be an effective way to keep learners tuned in! Just remember to write the question ahead of time and calculate where in the lesson you think it fits best.

Analyzing Classroom Practice

As principal of an elementary school, I had the opportunity to visit regularly in many classrooms. I shared with teachers my hope that the faculty would make a commitment to encouraging higher-level thinking on the part of students and that I would focus my observations in this area. I explained that I would be looking for two things:

1. Distribution of questions—*Are students consistently engaged and given sufficient opportunities to respond?*

2. Level or type of questions—*Are students challenged with higher-order questions?*

The teachers were very responsive. A second-grade teacher shared with me that she thought she was calling on boys much more than girls. Sure enough, when I observed her class and later tallied the distribution of questions, I saw that questions directed at boys outnumbered girls by two to one. Lack of wait time was also a factor; several times she called on a boy right away—primarily to get his attention.

In this teacher's case, the second-grade boys were irrepressible talkers and doers and the girls were bright, but compliant, students. She began to strategize right away on ways to counter her tendency—and she became very successful at bringing out the responses of her girls, while employing other strategies to engage her active boys.

I learned from observing this process that a classroom that is too well-managed might inadvertently undermine the encouragement of higher-order thinking. We need to adhere to our purpose for questioning, which is to develop students' thinking. Concerns about managing behavior should not compromise the quality of teaching.

ENCOURAGING CRITICAL THINKING

Daily opportunities should be provided for students to engage their brains beyond rote levels of recall. Richard Paul and Linda Elder from the Center for Critical Thinking assert, "The quality of our life and that of what we produce, make, or build depends precisely on the quality of our thought." Further, they say that critical thinking—the art of analyzing thinking with a view to improve it—must be systematically cultivated (2007, p. 4).

In the process of thinking, each of us looks through distinct lenses that serve as filters for the decisions, plans, and judgments we make. These personal filters subject our interpretation of information to our biases or distortions—a process that may result in ignorant

Raising Students' Awareness of Perspective and Bias

Students sometimes self-correct automatically, but guiding students through the process of acknowledging biases that color or stand in the way of the soundness of their reasoning should be directly, and carefully, taught. For example, if you've just read a story in which a key figure made a risky and unwise decision, you can use that scenario to elicit your students' thoughts on the biases of different characters. You might ask:

How would the character's father look at the action?

How would the character's favorite aunt look at the action?

How would the character's best friend look at the action?

How would the girl the character was trying to impress look at the action?

How would the girl's mother look at the action?

How would the character's younger brother look at the action?

How would the family doctor look at the action?

How would the town's minister look at the action?

How would the town's sheriff look at the action?

decisions or actions. As Paul and Elder suggest, true critical thinking is self-directed, self-disciplined, self-monitored, and self-corrected. In this state, we recognize and discard our biases, and engage in earnest communication and authentic efforts to solve problems.

If the following statements are lenses through which teachers gaze as they work with students, what are the underlying messages that they might be sending?

- I've been teaching low-track for five years and when my colleague retires, I want the advanced classes.

- I know this child struggles, but if I can have more time, I can get her to pass the writing test.

- Students these days just don't care about good literature.

- Once you meet his mom, you can understand why he acts the way he does.

- Don't let him get away with marginal work. He always tries to do the least amount of work, but if you hold his feet to the fire, he will produce.

- These kids aren't ready for higher-order thinking.

Just as teachers inadvertently communicate messages of high (or low) expectations, hope (or the lack thereof), bias, beliefs about the teacher's role, and a host of other perspectives, students also bring biases and misinformation to thinking. The effort to build critical-thinking skills doesn't necessarily eliminate these biases; rather, it makes us more aware of them and the fact that information can be tampered with because of our subjective way of experiencing the world. Thus, an aspect of metacognition (thinking about thinking) is to self-regulate and self-correct.

Reading Is Thinking

In one of my first education jobs, as an elementary reading specialist, I remember puzzled teachers coming to me saying, "He can read the words, but he can't recall anything he reads." We called these children—students who had never acquired strategies that support comprehension of literature and text—*word callers*. Laura Robb (2000) advises, "The purpose of reading becomes making meaning, a process that clarifies prior knowledge and enables readers to construct new understandings. To accomplish this, students have to be actively involved in understanding, using, and self-evaluating the effectiveness of reading strategies" (p.63). Every time a reader engages with text in a purposeful way higher-order comprehension strategies are employed. Our goal was to teach a repertoire of strategies to our teachers so they could teach them to their word callers!

Since learners spend so much time in school attempting to extract meaning from oral presentations or the written word, it is essential to examine higher-order thinking processes as they related to developing literacy. Seven key reading strategies that thoughtful readers use, outlined by Pearson, Roehler, Dole, and Duffy (1992), are intended to assist the reader in comprehending and thinking critically about a text. These seven strategies should be taught and practiced until they become part of the learner's repertoire:

1. **Activating background knowledge to make connections between new and known information**—How does what I know connect to what I am about to learn?

2. **Questioning the text**—Do I agree, disagree, have more questions?

3. **Drawing inferences**—What will happen next?

4. **Determining importance**—Which portion of the text should I remember?

5. **Creating mental images**—How can I improve my comprehension by tapping into visual memory systems?

6. **Repairing understanding when meaning breaks down**—I don't understand, so what "fix-it" strategy should I use?

7. **Synthesizing information**—How can I combine everything I've learned for greater meaning—connecting, questioning, and inferring to better understand?

As with teaching students about the brain and learning, comprehension strategies are most powerful when the terms associated with strategic reading are taught to students and they use the framework consistently—before, during, and after reading (see the Three-Part Reading Model, below). From the earliest school years and beyond, teachers need to communicate to students—consistently and in many different ways—the power of critical, strategic thinking. Opportunities to demonstrate this power must be incorporated into lesson design and daily practice.

Three-Part Reading Model

Some Strategies to Use Before Reading	**Some Strategies to Use During Reading**	**Some Strategies to Use After Reading**
These activate past knowledge and experiences	*These enable students to make personal connections, visualize, identify parts that confuse, monitor understanding, and recall information.*	*These enlarge past knowledge, deepen understanding and engagement with text, and can create connections to other texts.*
Brainstorm/Categorize	Make personal connections	Skim
Predict/Support	Use prior knowledge	Reread
Skim/Preview	Predict/Support/ Adjust/Confirm	Question
Pose questions	Pose questions	Visualize
Fast-Write	Identify confusing parts	Evaluate and adjust predictions
Preteach vocabulary	Visualize	Reflect through talking, writing, drawing
What do I know? What's new?	Self-monitor for understanding	Infer
Visualize/Recall other sensory experiences	Summarize	Compare/Contrast
	Synthesize	Cause and Effect
	Reread	Conclude
	Use context clues	Theme
	Infer	Note-taking
		Summarize
		Synthesize

"Three-Part Reading Model" © 2000 by Laura Robb, from *Teaching Reading in Middle School* (Scholastic).

Building Thinkers With Reciprocal Teaching

Another framework for supporting students' critical thinking is reciprocal teaching (Palincsar & Brown, 1984, 1986; Palincsar & Klenk, 1991). Based on initial research with seventh- and eighth-grade students with learning disabilities, Palincsar and her colleagues designed a model of teaching that emphasizes internal procedures readers use to self-regulate thinking as they read.

The teacher begins by modeling each of the segments, gradually turning over the reins to the students while providing feedback and encouragement. Implemented in triads (one teacher, two students), small groups, and regular classrooms, reciprocal teaching has been shown to bring about substantial gains in achievement. By expecting the students to act like teachers, four thinking strategies normally taught separately are combined in an instructional framework. These are mental strategies, so they are not visible, and therefore they are a challenge to teach. Students learn:

- **PREDICTING:** thinking about what they are preparing to read and making predictions

- **QUESTIONING:** developing self-questioning strategies

- **CLARIFYING:** recognizing and clarifying words and passages that they do not understand

- **SUMMARIZING:** summarizing or retelling passages after they read

The first step in the process is for the teacher to model each strategy with a think-aloud. A premise of reciprocal teaching is that a student's recall is enhanced when he or she verbalizes thinking and observes other students doing the same. Readers who do not understand how to do the think-aloud watch the teacher model the strategy, then practice it with support, and gradually begin to internalize the process for themselves. As with the other strategies, the teacher models the skill, then hands over the leadership responsibility to the students (Allen, 2003).

In Chapter 2, we talked about mirror neurons and how our brains mimic (or mirror) the actions of others. It follows that the requirement in reciprocal teaching to "act like the teacher" activates mirror neurons in students' brains. Not only are synaptic connections being reinforced in the sensory-motor mirroring of the teacher, but "empathetic" mirror neurons are also activated as students observe reciprocal teaching applied in a positive, supportive environment.

The teacher's role in this instructional process is fluid—ebbing and flowing with students' comfort and confidence levels. Reciprocal teaching is most successful when the teacher acts as an observer on the sidelines, providing some guidance, but allowing the students to effectively move through the four steps themselves. The teacher's ability to fill this role with confidence affects the learning process greatly.

Reciprocal teaching is most effective when it is applied as part of a comprehensive initiative to improve reading comprehension. Teachers should encourage students to use all four of the strategies before, during, and after reading to deepen their comprehension—not simply during reading instruction, but also when they're developing concepts in science, social studies, and math. Think-alouds and the process of taking turns being the teacher have proven to be very effective in helping students to focus on their learning and share their thinking about what they are learning, as well as in bonding students into a learning community (Hashey & Connors, 2003).

TEACHER AS FACILITATOR OF LEARNING

A theme of reciprocal teaching is that the teacher must become *dispensable,* letting the students do the work of thinking. It may sound strange, but the most powerful instruction is when teachers set the stage so the students are the players—not when the teacher is the "sage on the stage." This thread of constructing opportunities for students to do the work runs through all the frameworks discussed in this chapter. *Facilitator*, *guide-on-the-side*, *instructional coach*, *mentor*—each term sends a far different message than the the the all-too-frequent didactic approach of telling students what they need to know. The bottom line is, if we want students to grow as creative and critical thinkers, we must push them out of the proverbial nest and stop hand-feeding them the pacing guide content so they can spit it back on a test. To build the thinking capacities of our students, we must be intentional.

Getting It Right

I have always felt self-conscious about being videotaped as a teacher; however, I recognize the power of observing my own teaching and, most particularly, of noting the lost opportunities to turn questions around so *students* do the thinking. I now anticipate as I plan the lesson when a think-aloud will be helpful. Rather than simply accept a reply from students, I remember to ask them to tell me how they arrived at a response or request that they find evidence in the passage for answers they just gave. I work diligently on not lecturing, for I know how challenging it is for a teacher *not* to do most of the talking. I encourage and challenge each of you to monitor your own practice in this regard.

If we want students to develop as higher-order thinkers, we must tap into every available opportunity to make students do the work. And that work should get the brain's attention—through creativity, problem solving, choice, novelty, dissonance, movement, social interaction, and visual cues. As teachers, our smarter, brain-compatible lesson design includes these methods that engage students as critical and creative thinkers.

Reflection

1. Time yourself for three minutes: Complete a "quick-write" on everything you can think of that has to do with the brain and higher-order thinking. Check back in the chapter to see how you fared.

2. Complete the following table by identifying an example of how the activity or technique could be used at your grade level and/or content area:

Activity/Technique	How it could be used
Cinquain	_____
Somebody Wanted But So	_____
Divergent Questioning	_____
Reciprocal Teaching	_____

3. Select a class or subject area and complete the Building a Thinking Classroom survey (page 126) based on the students in that class. Discuss the results of your survey with a team member or colleague. Select two targets to work on as you design lessons that incorporate higher-order thinking.

4. Create a T-chart with a left-side heading of "My Students Do Well" and a heading of "My Students Can Work On" on the right. Review Robb's Three-Part Reading Model (page 86), and identify strategies in each column. Target a strategy in each column to develop with students.

5. **ACTIVATING PRIOR KNOWLEDGE (APK):** From a brain and learning perspective, list five or six insights that you have about why active learning helps students remember the targeted content.

Chapter 6

ENERGIZING THE BRAIN:
Movement, Music, and Social Interactions

A TALENTED, THOUGHTFUL teacher friend of mine was in the faculty workroom having a rather heartfelt conversation with a few colleagues about some particularly antsy students. She asked with genuine sympathy, "When it comes right down to it—could any of *us* sit for four or more hours a day, having an adult tell us what we need to know just to pass the test? We'd hate it!"

When she shared these comments with me, I cringed at how much her words applied to me. The truth is I'm sitting impaired. When forced to sit for too long, my foot constantly wiggles. In any meeting or at my desk, I frequently sit on the edge of my chair rocking almost imperceptibly as I work; I doodle elaborate geometric or paisley designs on napkins and notepads, and speakers' voices frequently compete with an ever-present song in my head. I sometimes wonder if I could "do" school again if the major mode of instruction required me to sit and listen.

My colleague's reflection is really a call to all teachers to think about the diversity and appropriateness of teaching methods. At the completion of every lesson, we should ask, "Were my students engaged as learners today?" Covering the content and meeting the pacing guide requirements amounts to very little if students aren't engaged. What should be comforting to classroom teachers is that we really do know how to design a lesson to keep students energized. Research on the brain and learning, particularly as it relates to the incorporation of movement, music, and social interactions into instruction on a regular basis, confirms how essential these learning experiences are for students.

The Importance of Engagement

When a teacher believes that direct or didactic instruction is the only way to convey information quickly and efficiently, what does it mean for the learner? We are always hopeful that the learners—despite a sit-and-listen approach—will absorb what is being taught. (Otherwise we wouldn't do it, right?) However, when the teacher does most of the talking, we get comments from students such as "This is boring. I am so tired of sitting and listening—if I could just put my head down and close my eyes." Truth be told, each of us has suffered through high school, college, and even workshop lectures with similar reactions. But when teachers plan for active engagement, what a difference for students—no heads

Adult Learners Struggle to Stay Focused, Too

Adult learners are able to sustain approximately 20–25 minutes of attention during a presentation or discussion. During workshops, every 20 minutes I try to change the manner in which I ask participants to pay attention —just to keep them engaged. Similarly, when training teachers, I emphasize the idea that "the brain can only tolerate what the backside can endure!" The fact is, teachers have the same trouble as students when asked to internalize meaningful content delivered in a sit-and-listen format!

on desks, few inattentive eyes, tuned-in students, minimal off-task behavior, a sense of energy, and yes, constructive noise in the environment.

A lack of engagement is the reason why many students seem to forget lessons from one day to the next. Teachers have shared with me the discouragement they feel when they teach a lesson one day—thinking it went very well—and the next day during a quick review, the students' faces seem so blank that it's as if the previous lesson hadn't occurred. Here's an illustration of the dilemma:

A history teacher reviewing the previous day's lesson asks his students, "Who recalls the significance of the Stamp Act?" No response. He tries again, "Why was December 16, 1773, important?" Once more no one responds—and many students look down at their desks. Still hopeful, he tries again, "What happened April 18, 1775?" Silence. Reaching a point of exasperation he sighs, "I talked about this material yesterday. Why can't you remember these events?" A young man in the back looks up and says with an equally emphatic sigh, "Because we weren't involved!"

What the young man means is that he wasn't involved in anything that occurred in the Revolutionary War period. From the perspective of many students, that's ancient history. However, his comment conveys an important message—for optimal learning and recall, students need to be engaged. If the previous day's instruction had been active—through role-play, simulation, music, visual arts, or even a You Were There writing activity—the students might have been able to remember that the Boston Tea Party occurred on December 16, 1773, and the night ride of Paul Revere was April 18, 1775. As you work on teaching smarter, be sure to capitalize on the benefits of involving students as active learners.

Moving to Learn: The Brain in Action

What happens in the brain when students are physically engaged in the learning task? Keep in mind that movement activates muscles and increases the involvement of the brain, directly influencing a student's ability to learn and remember (Ratey, 2001). Even moderate movement in the classroom, at recess and during physical education, will increase rates of blood flow in the brain. Similarly, small elevations of blood flow in the brain improve cognitive functioning because of an increase in necessary nutrients, such as oxygen and glucose (Etnier et al., 1997).

"Exercise improves learning on three levels: first, it optimizes your mind-set to improve alertness, attention, and motivation; second, it prepares and encourages nerve cells to bind to one another, which is the cellular basis for logging in new information; and third, it spurs the development of new nerve cells from stem cells in the hippocampus" (Ratey, 2008, p. 53). And there's more! Chemical alterations occur at the synapse when students are actively involved, tagging the content being learned so it can be accessed more readily when needed. Additionally, certain neurotransmitters that encode meaning are specifically

Exercise Builds Stronger Neural Networks

Figuring out more precisely how connections in the brain develop and grow has been a goal of neuroscientists for years. Ratey (2008) highlights the role of a family of proteins known as BDNF (brain-derived neurotrophic factor), which in the 1990s became a focus of a new line of research. It seems that neuro*transmitters* carry out signaling in the brain, while neuro*trophins* help develop and solidify the connections—a process Ratey calls "bolstering the infrastructure."

BDNF has been found to exist in the hippocampus—an area of the brain instrumental to memory and learning. The hippocampus works in collaboration with the executive prefrontal cortex, which examines stimuli and creates order and meaning out of the incoming information. Thus the hippocampus links with the cerebellum and basal ganglia. Adding exercise to the mix increases BDNF in the brain, which in turn strengthens neural networks. When physical activity increases in complexity—not just running 30 minutes a day on a treadmill, but through mixed workouts or aerobics—greater amounts of BDNF are found to be present in the cerebellum. The more BDNF, the stronger the connections for enhancing memory and learning.

influenced by physical activity. For example, increased levels of norepinephrine, serotonin, and endorphins have been found in the brain after a period of physical exercise. In fact, there is evidence exercise may have long-term effects on norepinephrine levels, and high levels of this neurotransmitter have been associated with improved memory (Ruch, 2001).

Teaching With Movement in Focus

The bottom line for teachers is that with physical activity, students' muscles and brains are exercised and their ability to retrieve memories associated with the movement is enhanced. Think of it as "Happy feet, happy brain!" Ratey explains, "visiting a new place, seeing a movie, singing a new song, or solving a new problem are all ways to stimulate the brain. In each instance movement is a major player in learning" (2001, p. 179). For example, let's go back to the map of the United States on the library floor (as described in Chapter 4). When taking a history quiz, a student's subconscious connection between movement and learning might be, "I can answer the question about Lewis and Clark's expedition because I remember walking the Missouri River on the giant map on the floor of the library."

What else do we know about the role of movement in improving academic performance and memory? Eric Jensen, a crusader for applying brain research in the classroom, acknowledges that simply standing up can increase the heart rate, and thus, increase blood flow to the brain, boosting thinking. Jensen notes that students get bored sitting, and when energy is lagging, students should stand up (1995). An example you might use after a mini-lecture is to say to students: "On your own, write down three important things you learned in the mini-lesson, then stand, find a partner for an SSS—standing share session—and compare your responses."

BACKWARD THINKING: DIMINISHING PHYSICAL ACTIVITY

"Can you believe our school has reduced PE to two days a week to build in more math time?" These words came from an amazing physical education teacher I know, who adeptly weaves academic standards—including math—into her PE classes. Her job was secure, but a less-experienced colleague lost her job because a position was eliminated.

Administrators are often forced to make difficult decisions about which sections of the curriculum can be eliminated or shortened to make room for more reading, writing, and arithmetic—and unfortunately more practice taking "the test." With increasing frequency, administrators and school boards are making ill-advised decisions to cut out physical education, reduce recess, and revert to pacing guides so jam-packed that activities that engage students are seen as nonessential, icing on the cake. Art and music classes are equally vulnerable.

Cutting the very programs that enhance learning and recall—art, music, and physical education—cannot be credited only to bureaucratic decisions. Some schools and teachers have classroom management policies that aim to modify student behavior by using recess as leverage against students who are acting out in class—for every tally mark against the student, another five minutes of recess is eliminated.

A New Trend?

Curiously, the concern about the obesity epidemic among young people is becoming an impetus to add or hold onto physical education classes and recess. The by-product of this push to exercise may well be students who are more ready to learn.

Aren't these students the very ones who need the movement? Isn't physical exercise correlated with cognitive growth? How confusing for well-intended teachers to send such mixed messages. Many teachers I know compensate by building movement into daily lesson plans—recess or not! However, no teacher should have to be secretive about providing opportunities for students to be physically active, and all teachers should design lessons to actively engage students.

The evidence is too strong that exercise and movement influence learning. As you support restoration of recess and physical education, make sure your colleagues understand the brain research regarding movement and its impact on learning in the classroom. In the same vein, advocate for physical education programs that focus on wellness and helping students attain their personal best. Ratey (2008) cites programs in Naperville Central High, west of Chicago, and Titusville, Pennsylvania, where physical education classes have been transformed and fully integrated into the academic learning goals of the schools. These exemplary programs don't have to be exceptions!

Making the Most of Seatwork Time

Teachers often struggle to plan meaningful seatwork that keeps students suitably engaged when the teacher is working with a small group. If the optimal time for sustained activity is approximately the learner's age, what actions should you take to teach smarter when it comes to grouping?

Using the age formula, a fifth-grade teacher knows that many students working on their own will start getting antsy after 10–12 minutes. When designing the lesson, the question she needs to ask herself is, "If I want twenty minutes with the group at my reading table, can I use movement of some kind to shift the attention state of the students doing seatwork so they stay on task?" The trick is to set up the lesson to avoid tedium as well as the "I'm finished early so I'll daydream" mind-set. Teachers have shared the following examples of strategies to keep students engaged:

- After completing a notebook task at their desks, students shift their focus by working with partners or small groups on a related activity, preferably in a new location.

- After working on a word-sort assignment with a partner at the same level, students go to their reading baskets to select a familiar leveled reader or a novel they are reading to search for words that have features similar to the words in the sort.

- After asking students to work in pairs to complete an A-to-Z Review organizer on any word or phrase related to the topic they are studying, students return to their desks and write two paragraphs on the topic, using their responses on the A-to-Z as prompts. Adding illustrations introduces another modality.

There is nothing earth-shattering about these strategies, so they are quite doable. The art of successful seatwork time is to plan for physical movement and attention shifts for students so they are constantly engaged in meaningful work!

Keeping Students on Task

Tracy Gunn, an eighth-grade English teacher, is masterful at using a variety of focus/ refocus shifts to keep her students engaged. "English teacher" is really a misnomer—Tracy sees her job as guiding literacy so her students, whom she refers to as "ladies and gentle-men," can become outstanding readers and writers. Not only does she understand how to build a literacy-rich classroom, she truly gets smart lesson design. The timing of her lessons reflects the need for 13-year-old eighth graders to change their physical and atten-tive states every 11–15 minutes.

Tracy weaves movement, music, and cooperative tasks seemingly effortlessly into one day's lesson. Management issues are minimal, and she deals with them in a low-key way that focuses high expectations on her students. For example, when one young man put his head on his desk, within three seconds, Tracy responds with a firm, but non-caustic "Head up, or please stand up, sir," and the student complies immediately, with no negativity. Tracy had clearly outlined her behavioral expectations, and a head on the desk was not acceptable.

The outline on the following page illustrates how the 55-minute integrated literacy lesson was organized to engage and instruct learners, with the teacher as the guide and students doing the work.

MINUTES	ENGAGEMENT	LESSON COMPONENT
5	Reflection: on your own or with desk partners	The task is for students to analyze the dialogue in a text selection and respond to the open-ended question "What tools did the author use to help you follow the conversations?" They are given one page of dialogue from a Harry Potter book and asked to circle clues on this sheet that answer the question and, on a separate piece of paper, describe the elements they circled.
10	Whole-class debrief	On chart paper, Tracy summarizes students' reflections about their dialogues. She solicits responses, requiring students who have not already responded to give feedback. She has a strong sense of *wait time* and appropriately affirms their responses.
2	Movement break: rhythm, chant	When a student mentions the tool "punctuation before quotation," Tracy asks the class to stand up and models a chant—marching her feet while snapping her fingers saying, "Punctuation, then quotation." When a student makes the chant really jazzy, she lets him sit down, encouraging other students to get into it. When half the class is down, she lets the whole class sit down. Students are energized and giggling a bit about moving with the beat.
3	Transition: independent	Tracy gives students a few minutes to place their dialogue sheets in literacy binders. She checks with students to see if they know the section the papers should go in. They do.
12	Whole-class location change	Tracy asks the class to move to the back carpet for a shared reading selection as a model for writing. Most students move to the rug; a few bring chairs around. Tracy sits in a rocker and explains that she is reading a selection that focuses on text-to-self reflections.
5	Transition: independent task	Transition back to desks. Tracy asks students to get out their notebooks and, if they're interested in the themes just discussed from the shared story, add them to the writing "territories" (topics that are meaningful to individual students that might be used as a writing theme in the future) section in their notebooks.

12	Cooperative groups: triads	Tracy explains that students are now to work in cooperative groups. The goal is to acknowledge a few topics from writing territories that they have written down and to share several things that made that territory—or theme—a potential writing topic. Tracy allows students to group themselves, but cautions them that they will be able to self-select groups again only if they include everyone. Students group themselves quickly and inclusively to maintain the privilege. Tracy walks around the room briefly listening in and interacting with students in triads.
6	Journal writing	Tracy asks students to respond in their journals to the question: "How do you feel about reading and writing in this classroom after two weeks of school?" She puts on instrumental background music and walks around giving quiet feedback as students are writing.

Obviously, Tracy's class is not a physical education class; however, during her time with students, she consciously involves them by building in activities that incorporate physical activity and adjusts activities so different states of learning are activated. Her strategies include the following:

- Variety of interactions: teacher-led, working on their own, with a partner, and cooperative groups
- Changing venues: desk, rug, cooperative group, self-selected location
- Using energizers: rhythm chant, background music
- Building in choice: grouping themselves, students select potential writing topics to share

LEARNING WITH MUSIC

Movement and music are intertwined in the brain. I am particularly interested in learning through music because music is my avocation. Though you may deplore the double negative, I tell people, "I can't *not* have music in my life!" The a capella singing found in many compositions from the 10th through the 16th century soothes and energizes my spirit. Think of it. Well over 500 years ago, composers had no technology other than quill pens and ink on paper, and yet they wrote eight-part harmonies that truly define the word *sublime*!

Though my personal taste in music may not be everyone's cup of tea, the inclination to respond to rhythm and music extends to almost everyone. We tap our feet to our favorite types of music, whether bluegrass, blues, R&B, salsa, country, or good ol' rock & roll. Swaying to slow dance tunes or gentle new age rhythms occurs naturally. In fact, when music plays, the motor areas of a listener's brain activate, even when he or she is not moving (Jhamandas, 2002)—it seems that music calls to us!

Music and the Brain: A Biology Moment

Daniel Levitan, a rocker-turned-neuroscientist, writes elegantly about how brains and music coevolved: "The story of your brain on music is the story of an exquisite orchestration of brain regions, involving both the oldest and newest parts of the human brain, and regions as far apart as the cerebellum in the back of the head and the frontal lobes just behind your eyes" (2006). Initial processing of music happens in the auditory cortex. Frontal lobes analyze the structure and evaluate expectations, perhaps asking, "Why music, why now?" The nucleus accumbens activates when the music is deemed pleasurable, which influences dopamine production. Meanwhile, the "old-brain" cerebellum helps mediate it all—pulse, rhythm, meter, and movement—connecting to the frontal lobe and limbic system (Levitan, 2006).

Music is a remarkable encoding device. Our brains remember events and information that are musically tagged! In an experiment, people who were randomly stopped on the

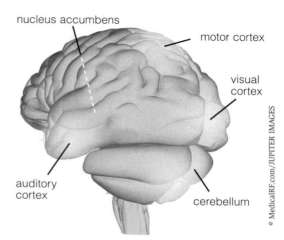

nucleus accumbens
motor cortex
visual cortex
auditory cortex
cerebellum

© MedicalRF.com/JUPITER IMAGES

Key areas of the brain responsible for listening, viewing, and moving

Music—Stimulant and Stressor

Both singing and listening to music prompt a chemical shift that results in an increased sense of pleasure or well-being. Music encodes strongly because it triggers the reward centers in the brain, activating the neurotransmitter dopamine, which is associated with responses that to us seem rewarding (Jhamandas, 2002). Additionally, serotonin levels are higher at times when music is perceived to be pleasant as opposed to unpleasant. Dissonant music can actually cause distress—reduced serotonin levels; whereas, music perceived as pleasurable inhibits the reuptake of serotonin—keeping it in the brain longer (Evers & Suhr, 2000).

Insights About Music and Learning

The effect of music on listeners has been touted through the centuries. Perhaps the individuals making the statements below knew something about the brain and music. Let's draw some parallels between a few famous quotes and their implications for the classroom:

> "Where words fail, music speaks."
>
> HANS CHRISTIAN ANDERSEN

Music *speaks*—brings meaning—when the content is embedded in familiar songs and rhythms. Recall also improves when students associate a part of the lesson with music or when music is used to express the mood or setting of a story or event.

> "Music hath charms to soothe the savage beast."
>
> JAMES BRAMSTON

Selected background music can calm students in a classroom and focus their attention on learning tasks. Music can also energize or assist in increasing productivity.

> "Music is the medicine of the mind."
>
> JOHN LOGAN

When listening to music that is not dissonant, the brain has a chemical response increasing levels of dopamine and serotonin in the brain—with a corresponding sense of pleasure or calm. In this vein, music fosters an increased sense of well-being.

street were asked to sing a popular song entirely from memory, Levitan found that the two-thirds of the people were surprisingly accurate in pitch and most were on target in tempo, to the degree that when the recording of the subject singing was played next to the original song—it sounded like a sing-along.

The same thing happens when we are driving down the highway listening to an oldies station and a familiar song is played. We not only sing along to the tune, but we recall words that we may not have sung for years. I played Cat Stevens every night in my freshman year of college to block out noise on the dorm hall—and I remember every cut on the record! Many songs stimulate visual recall as well—high school gatherings, prom dances, football games, singing around the campfire, or end-of-summer romances. As soon as the music begins, we are transported back to the event, the people, even the *feel* of the moment.

Another illustration of the potency of music as an aid for recollection is found in the fact that only a modest stimulus is needed to help us recall an entire musical phrase or song. In the old TV game show *Name That Tune*, contestants competed to see who could recognize a song first, with as few notes as possible. It was amazing how brief a prompt some of the contestants needed. Similarly, if you have ever observed music fans at a concert, they often start celebrating the song that is about to be played after hearing only a few chords or notes. Our brains complete the musical phrase—and frequently the whole song—because it has been seared into memory.

The cerebellum—the part of the brain that helps coordinate automatic movement—is a key component of our perception of rhythm and music. It synchronizes the pulse or rhythm of a selection—speeding up and slowing down with the music and anticipating the next musical phrase. If the phrase is unconventional or reflects a surprising turn in the music, the cerebellum adjusts for the unexpected twist in pulse or rhythm (Levitan, 2006).

When we listen to music, other motor areas of the brain become active, as well. Our fingers tap the table, our body moves to the music, our head nods to the beat, and we smile with recognition of the rhythm or tune—in short, we engage more of our brain.

Teaching Smarter With Music in Focus

Music can be a dynamic tool to help students learn content for the end-of-week quiz or end-of-class standards test. Since positive music stimulation is associated with increases in both dopamine and serotonin levels *and* since these neurotransmitters boost encoding of information, I encourage teachers to find ways to effectively incorporate music into the classroom. In *The Learning Brain* (1995), Eric Jensen provides the following guidance:

> Use music carefully and purposefully for best effect. Too much can create saturation to the listener, and it loses its effectiveness. As a general rule, include music in 30% or less of the total learning time, unless the class requires it by nature of its content. The artful use of music can educate, heal, inspire, boost learning and build confidence. (p. 213)

Using music *purposefully* is the key. Up-front lesson design allows a teacher to consider at what point in a lesson and for what purpose music should be built in. The following think-alouds illustrate circumstances for which you might incorporate music:

- I have been teaching a 10-minute lesson on plant anatomy to my third graders, and I'll shift their attention states by having them stand up and sing the content words "Roots and stems, leaves and flowers" to the tune and motions of "Heads and Shoulders, Knees and Toes" after the mini-lesson.

- I am introducing a social studies lesson on ancient Greece and Rome and want to have some grand music playing as students walk into the room after library class. I remember when I was in band and played the trumpet section in "The Great Gate of Kiev" from Mussorgsky's *Pictures at an Exhibition*. I'll play a recording of that piece to set the stage as students are walking in the classroom.

- My students are reading two Caldecott Honor stories about Native Americans of the Southwest—*When Clay Sings* and *The Desert Is Theirs*. I have some flute music played by a Native American artist from Arizona that would complement the stories if I play it softly in the background.

- I want my seventh-grade math students to write lyrics about solving equations, so I'm going to have them work with a partner and make up new lyrics to a common tune. I wrote one as an example, to the tune of "Are you Sleeping?" ("Frère Jacques"):

    Learn equations, learn equations

    Always balancing, always balancing

    Solving operations

    Both sides treated fairly

    Finding solutions, finding solutions.

- Students in cooperative learning groups often get restless and off focus. I'll put on a rhythmic CD and we'll do a two-minute movement-and-music interval before they get back to work.

- I want students to write in their journals for ten minutes, so I will put on my *Music for Productivity* CD (Arcangelos Chamber Ensemble, 1998), which provides gentle classical music at 60 beats per minute, to help them focus.

Music Resources for Teachers

MUSIC FOR LEARNING   www.advancedbrain.com

MUSIC FOR THE CLASSROOM   www.intelli-tunes.com/whatsnew.htm

LEARNING FROM LYRICS   http://artsedge.kennedy-center.org/content/2058/

SINGING THE STANDARDS   www.singingthestandards.com

Getting Students on Board

Younger students tend to be very responsive to silly or fun songs that support the content to be learned, but middle school learners benefit from music in lessons, as well. However, since students at this age struggle with the "coolness factor," teachers may have to be more creative when adding music. Tish Moore, a sixth-grade math teacher, reports that she regularly uses music and movement to reinforce math concepts:

Music and rhythm are an essential part of my mathematics instruction. Using music often doubles as a form of classroom management—as in these examples where it supports transitioning from one task to another:

"When the music starts, begin the following tasks . . ."

"Complete this task before the music ends. . . ."

I also combine teaching patterns and sequences with a classroom management technique by using the following chant.

If you can hear me clap your hands once. (clap)

If you can hear me clap your hands twice. (clap, clap)

If you can hear me clap this rhythm. (rhythmic clap)

I use different types of music to calm or even excite my students. I find that tempo correlates with class pacing. I also use music for direct instruction and for memory devices. I take commonly known songs and change the lyrics to suit my needs in the classroom. We sing many songs, such as "Same, Change, Change" (to the tune of "Chain of Fools") to help us remember the algorithm for dividing fractions, and "The Properties Song" (to the tune of "YMCA") for recalling the characteristics of each mathematical property.

Any time I use music or rhythm in my classroom, I try to pair it with movement or dance. For example, we often use "Decimal Division Dance Party," a combination of music and dance to complete division problems with decimals. Multiplication hip-hop CDs are also popular.

I constantly search for current music to use to enhance my standards. Music and rhythm are essential parts of my teaching and my classroom climate.

Making the Case for Social Interaction

When working with middle school teachers, I often ask, "Why do middle school students come to school?" They always laugh, responding, "To be with their friends!" "What?" I retort, "Not to learn about physical science, or North American explorers, or multiplying fractions?" Teachers are aware that students' desire to interact with friends often interrupts their ability to attend to the lesson. So why not capitalize on the need for social interaction when designing lessons? Social and emotional competence is a key to positive interactions with friends and adults, and later success in life. Gaining proficiency in these areas helps students manage "life tasks such as learning, forming relationships, solving everyday problems, and adapting to the complex demands of growth and development" (Elias et al., 1997, p. 2).

Actively Learning Social Skills

At Central High in Naperville, Illinois, a mandatory square dancing class was added for all freshman. The physical activity and learning complexity of the square dance steps was one goal. Another was to help students develop skills in talking to each other. Partners used scripts designed to foster conversations in interactions that increased in length, culminating in a 15-minute conversation. A final exam asked students to recall ten facts about their partner. In a fun, nonthreatening gym-class environment, students gained confidence in skills of conversation that carried beyond the classroom (Ratey, 2008).

Students who struggle in school often have marginal skills in social interaction. Research on risk and resiliency highlights factors that influence why one child manages to move beyond a demonstrably at-risk situation, while another child living next door ends up in a series of encounters with the law and with seemingly no chance of breaking the cycle. Both have similar home environments and neighborhoods—so what is the difference? Key factors that support the success of at-risk learners include social competence, autonomy, problem solving, and the presence of a significant adult in the life of the student (Henderson & Milstein, 2003). These four factors relate significantly to skills in social interaction:

SOCIAL COMPETENCE: The student knows how to interact appropriately and constructively with adults and peers.

AUTONOMY: The student thinks for him- or herself and does not have to be driven by "groupthink."

PROBLEM SOLVING: The student doesn't have a meltdown when confronted with concerns or problems, rather he or she knows how to ask for help and search out solutions independently.

SIGNIFICANT ADULT: The student has an advocate or mentor to encourage, guide, prod, support, and believe in his or her ability to succeed.

BUILDING A CARING CLASSROOM

Our brains have an innately social disposition. When you think how humankind has survived over the eons, it is clear that community is a critical factor. When people traveled together and shared food and lodging, it supported the notion of "safety in numbers." Even in recent decades, front-porch discussions were the way that many people kept up with the news, the gossip, and socializing. Before the rampant use of personal technology devices, families and friends interacted chiefly through conversation, music, games, and even shared reading of books or newspapers.

It may seem that I am longing for the good ol' days, but my real intent is to point out how opportunities for socialization both in families and communities have diminished—leaving schools largely responsible for filling the gap. Ratey has this to say about the power of socialization, "Our highest human virtue is our connection with other humans, and social activity is basic to our health and happiness. Our brains are preprogrammed to look for other humans from the moment of birth, and continuing social interaction with parents and peers is essential for normal development throughout life" (2001, p. 297).

Successful socialization in a classroom or school depends on each student feeling cared about—by both teachers and peers. To build resiliency, we must strengthen a student's bond to the school environment. Many disenfranchised students have little or no sense of such a bond, neither with other students nor with the adults in the building. If caring—a value that enriches our lives—is rooted in the social and emotional development of children, then teachers should consciously build caring relationships with students. What is encouraging is that social competence can be developed—through modeling, observing something done properly, practicing interactions, and scripting possible responses.

SOCIALIZING AND THE BRAIN

Socializing is profoundly tied up with emotions. How does our brain respond as we interact with others? When we have a positive social interaction that warms us and makes us feel involved with the group, the processing seems to occur in the left frontal lobe. In contrast, if experiences are negative, evoking distrust or sadness, the right frontal lobe is principally involved in the processing (Ratey, 2008).

When confronted with a highly charged emotional situation, the amygdala will signal a response to the nearby hypothalamus to respond appropriately—flight, fight, or freeze! The amygdala also plays a role in consolidating long-term memories with a positive or negative emotional tag. For example, I still remember a situation in which my kindergarten teacher made me go to the back of the line after our end-of-the-day recess because she said I was pushing. Of course, I thought she was terribly wrong and unfair. Not only did I go to the back of the line, but I hid behind the garbage cans on the side of the school until my older brothers came out of school—never even going back into class. Obviously, this negative memory is etched into my brain.

Powerful stress hormones, such as cortisol, are released when life's challenges become overwhelming. If cortisol—and other related hormones—remain too high for extended periods, people may suffer from increased heart disease, suppressed immune functions, exacerbated diabetes and hypertension, and possible destruction of neurons in the hippocampus—harming memory (Goleman, 1996). What this means for teachers is that when students are highly stressed, the oversecretion of cortisol can physically deteriorate key areas of factual memory and reflective systems (Sylwester, 2005). In short, stress can inhibit learning and recall.

Although the stress response initially evolved because of physical dangers, much of the stress students experience today stems from perceived social challenges that don't require the flight-or-fight response (Sylwester, 2005). As we noted in Chapter 1, stressful situations abound in school. When sides are picked for the kickball game, how does it feel to the ones picked last? What about the students who sit alone at lunch or end up eating with the one or two other isolates from the class? When students group themselves, which students never get picked or end up in someone's group by default. These students know very well that no one jumped up and said, "Be in my group."

Daniel Goleman (1996) describes how relationships affect both experience and biology. "The brain-to-brain link allows our strongest relationships to shape us on matters as benign as whether we laugh at the same jokes or as profound as which genes are (or are not) activated in T-cells, the immune system's foot soldiers in the constant battle against invading bacteria and viruses. That link is a double-edged sword: nourishing relationships have a beneficial impact on our health, while toxic ones can act like slow poison in our bodies" (p. 281).

The importance of relationships, whether nourishing or toxic, is evident in studies on how relationships affect achievement. Studies have found that when teachers showed warmth and positive regard toward students, and the culture of the class was nurturing and pleasant, students in both first and fifth grade performed at higher levels. In contrast, struggling students who were taught by a cold, controlling teacher continued to struggle—

even if appropriate academic strategies were in play (Goleman, 1996). Thus, even a technically strong teacher will have lower gains in achievement if the students view him or her as uncaring.

Incorporating Socialization in Lesson Design

Our students—all of them—want to feel cared about. Struggling learners particularly need to have a sense of belonging. How can we encourage socialization and caring in our classrooms? Clearly, if students thrive on positive interactions with others, teachers should create opportunities for those interactions to occur. I suggest the following three ways to do so:

- Develop a systematic process for promoting students' social and emotional learning skills.

- Highlight social and emotional learning skills embedded in the content you are teaching.

- Build positive social interactions into daily lessons with corresponding instructional tasks.

Schools can promote social skills through staff-designed programs or packaged programs such as Character Counts (2001). When I was an elementary school principal, the faculty and staff studied the idea of building resiliency in students. As part of the process, we identified life skills (Kovalik & Olsen, 1997) that we wanted to teach students, and decided to focus on one skill a month. For example, in October we studied the life skill of perseverance; one second-grade class performed a skit, another class came up with a song, and the third class delivered morning announcements. Faculty committees planned the events, created bulletin boards, and wrote letters to parents that highlighted the emphasized life skill—everyone was on board.

In the same vein, one middle school I visited dealt with the problem of bullying by conducting workshops for students and placing anti-bullying posters all over the building. Many middle schools set aside time each day for all students to participate in small advisory groups overseen by a teacher or staff member who encourages dialogue and open exchanges. Ratey (2001) points out that even 15 minutes a week can help children learn how to be friends, how to recognize and talk about different feelings, how to handle anger or pain, and how to express what they like and dislike.

Another way to help students gain insight into social skills is to select content that models the concept. Here are some examples:

RESPONSIBILITY: Write a letter to the editor of your local newspaper voicing your concerns about pollution in the local stream. (*Science*)

DECISION-MAKING SKILLS, PROBLEM SOLVING: Imagine you are a reporter writing a news article after interviewing a historical figure about a key incident in history, such as Abraham Lincoln writing the Emancipation Proclamation. Consider the following: What did this person need to consider when making decisions? What groups of people were involved? What processes did he or she use to come to conclusions? (*U.S. history*)

COMPROMISE, ORGANIZATION, MEETING A DEADLINE: As part of health class, your fifth grade has been given the chance to create the lunch menu for a full week. Poll students and come to a conclusion on the five meals you recommend. (*Health*)

EMPATHY, CARING, FLEXIBILITY: In the book you are reading, consider a character who is in trouble. Write a letter to that character that offers some possible solutions to the situation as well as some encouragement. Show in your letter that you are a person who cares. (*English*)

Cooperative Learning Strategies

Teachers have a great deal of autonomy in deciding how to weave movement and social interaction into lessons; yet, even though cooperative learning techniques are familiar to most teachers, they are often underutilized. With the reassurance that learning can be enhanced through well-structured social interactions, we can push their use to the forefront.

An example of cooperative learning in action is evident in a lesson about the rock cycle created by teacher Stephanie Haskins. She had her students work on one of three rock groups—igneous, sedimentary, or metamorphic—to become an "expert." After receiving a name tag representing their rock group, the students sat in a circle and then followed this procedure, described by Haskins:

> Have students gather in a circle so that each rock type is grouped together. Explain to students that they will be passing their beanbag (representing their type of rock) to a person with a different rock type. They must state the reason the rock changes as they pass the beanbag. (Provide an example.) Explain to students that they will continue passing the beanbag until everyone has had a chance to pass it. Students must remember the first person they passed to, since the beanbag activity will continue through a second cycle.

Cooperative learning activities can be easily structured and readily attached to class content. Groupings may be *formal* (lasting for a period of days or weeks through an assigned task), *informal* (occurring for a few minutes or a portion of the class), or *base groups* (long-term groups that have stable membership over a semester or year).

Ideas on assigning students to groups and structures for interaction are found in numerous sources (Johnson, Johnson, & Holubec, 1994; Kagan, 1994; Slavin, 1995). In

Carousel Brainstorming

Carousel brainstorming is a technique that uses a cooperative learning model to increase fluency of thinking. The class is arranged in teams of four to six students. Questions or prompts have been placed around the room on large poster sheets—one question per sheet. For example, in a science lesson on the solar system and space exploration, the prompts might include:

- Write down words that might be used in an article about the solar system.

- Identify things that exist in space.

- List names of people who have contributed to our understanding of the solar system.

- Identify scientific terms that pertain to any aspect of space flight.

Each team is given a different-colored magic marker and asked to stand in front of one of the poster sheets. When the signal is given, the first team member responds to the question in front of him or her, then passes the magic marker to the next team member to respond, and so on. until time is called (approximately one to two minutes per station). As an alternative, team members can confer, with a single recorder writing responses.

After about two minutes, time is called and each team rotates clockwise to the next poster and responds to the question. The new group may not duplicate a response already on the sheet. (Because each team has a different-colored magic marker, it is easy to see the number of answers each team has given.)

> Write down words that might be
> used in an article about the solar system.
>
> | | | |
> |---|---|---|
> | sun | shooting stars | orbit |
> | Saturn | rocket | planets |
> | Mars | satellite | crater |
> | Venus | space shuttle | launch |
> | Pluto | launch | ~~Space Shuttle~~ |
> | Jupiter | radar | earth |
> | Neptune | telescope | Apollo 13 |
> | Uranus | Space Shuttle | stardust |
> | | Mars Rover | Big Dipper |
> | meteor | Star Wars | Little Dipper |
> | asteroid | Star Trek | robot |
> | stars | | |
> | black hole | moons | |
> | Milky Way | sunspots | |
> | comets | gravity | |

structured cooperative learning, observers may use an observation form to indicate how well the group works together. Ideally, the class helps develop the form. A clearer picture of the social interaction within a group results when observers take note of who contributes ideas, who listens, who encourages participation, and who provides direction. Teachers can use observation responses to coach students.

Less formal strategies involve partner or triad activities in which a teacher asks students to turn to a nearby peer or peer group and work collaboratively to come up with responses. A Think-Pair-Share format may have students writing responses on their own, comparing notes with another student, and finally, sharing the merged responses with the whole class. A variation on the theme is Think-Pair-Square, in which two students then partner with two more students to have a broader exchange.

Other cooperative learning activities, such as the Jigsaw II technique, break up the content to be learned and ask students to become experts on one part of the assigned information or text. As students interact in their "expert" group, they employ social skills as they work toward a common goal. Later on, students from each expert group teach what they've learned to the whole class. Carousel brainstorming (see page 108) is another technique that utilizes both movement and cooperative interaction.

Numerous cooperative learning techniques are available to teachers in text and online. Selecting the one most appropriate for students, the content you teach, and the purpose of the lesson is something you'll need to decide upon during the lesson design. Any strategy that requires students to work collaboratively toward a common goal will help develop skills in social interaction. Remember to model the strategies and set ground rules for interaction so no students are blindsided.

Building Community in the Classroom

Watching teachers at faculty meetings is always interesting. If you were a fly on the wall at these meetings, you would observe interactions remarkably similar to those in your classroom. You would see the talkers, the snackers, the fringe listeners, who laugh at the exchanges yet say very little, those who are a little too loud—or a little too frustrated, the ones who were having a bad day before they even got to school. You'd see those who see the glass as half full and those who don't. You would see some who always come prepared, some who did the work but left it behind, and the ones who never even got to the task. A faculty meeting is a slice of the total school community, where diverse people interact on many levels. As much as teachers may not want another meeting, the social interaction in a faculty meeting is engaging because there is energy in a community.

One of the reasons professional learning communities are encouraged is because they generate enthusiasm and a sense of ownership—accomplishments that top-down efforts rarely achieve. Learning communities are self-regulated and are considered to be strong entities through which growth and progress can be facilitated (Dufour, Eaker, & Dufour, 2005).

Similarly, learning communities offer students the opportunities to participate in their own growth. Students and teachers need to act as partners in figuring out the best ways to successfully meet learning targets. Let students take part in planning and even delivering instruction. Create opportunities—and in turn, increase responsibility—for students to plan their learning. The very process of participating more in the decisions about instruction will improve socialization skills, but of course, the main objective is to have productive classroom learning communities where positive social interaction helps both students and teachers thrive.

The phrase "just do it" is common in today's make-it-happen culture. The truth is that when it comes to incorporating movement, music, and social interaction as part of the everyday classroom experience for students, we should *just do it!* In that regard, I encourage you to just do the following:

- Design movement into each lesson, knowing how students' brains grow when exercise and physical activity are an integral part of classroom instruction.

- Use music to boost recall and create an environment that engages both the learner's emotions and attention.

- Build in social interaction and cooperative learning strategies to develop skills of working effectively with others, to counter isolation, and to provide students with opportunities to learn from one another.

Reflection

1. Consider a lesson that you will teach in the next two weeks. Outline the lesson and select appropriate times when you can add music to adjust the attention states of the learners. Share this lesson design with a colleague to get feedback.

2. Dopamine and serotonin increase when music is used in the classroom. Review what happens when these neurotransmitters are activated. When you next incorporate music, observe and write down responses students have during the activity. Are they energized, soothed, or more attentive? Is acting-out behavior reduced?

3. Describe how you know when your students need to start moving. How do you incorporate, or could you incorporate, movement to keep your students engaged?

4. Describe a few ways that the music, art, and/or physical education teachers at your school have integrated content objectives into their classes. Highlight any techniques you think you can use to enhance your lessons.

5. Use the Internet to identify three to four new cooperative learning strategies to use with your students. Build one of these strategies into a lesson design. The following Web site provides some helpful links: www.thirteen.org/edonline/concept2class/month5/index_sub2.html.

6. **ACTIVATING PRIOR KNOWLEDGE (APK):** Setting targets is a key to growth. Identify five ways you plan to incorporate brain-compatible strategies into your teaching.

CONCLUSION:
Putting Brain-Compatible Instruction Into Practice

HOW DO WE "teach smarter" and help our students become more capable, self-motivated learners? We commit daily to teaching with a focus on the learning brain—and modeling our practices so others can do so, as well. I've worked with a number of teachers at the grassroots level and have seen how student by student, teacher by teacher, school by school dramatic change can happen. Let me leave you with eight considerations to help you get there from here:

- Embrace best practice

- Establish instructional look-fors

- Make a "stop doing" list

- Identify passionate champions

- Acknowledge colleagues who are on board

- Involve students and other stakeholders

- Stick to the message

- Audit your practice

Embrace Best Practice

As a guest teacher, I recently discussed with a group of high school seniors the variety of teaching styles and instructional formats they had experienced in their school careers. I asked them to respond in writing to the question "In the nearly four years since you started high school, what have teachers done that help you learn best?"

Here are a few of their responses:

- "Teachers interact with students and that helps me learn. Teachers can't just give out work sheets and expect us to learn and remember. We need hands-on and group activities so that we get involved and are not so bored. Not . . . all the time, but a lot of times."

- "Teachers help me learn best when they are being more hands on, interesting, explaining in depth. Also, giving visual images of what they are speaking of."

- "Teachers help me learn when they take time and make sure you understand what they are saying and when they make sure the information becomes real in the way we can use it in everyday life. Groups are good, but not all the time."

- "I just really despise lecturing from up front and taking notes. I like teachers to get on a more respectful level with students and become part of the class—being less the superior."

Seventeen of the 18 responses expressed a desire for hands-on work, visual prompts, group interaction, teachers who relate to them, and making the information relevant. Throughout this book, we've discussed the very strategies that students requested. These responses were from seniors, but I have no doubt that students at many other levels would express similar hopes. The bottom line is to make brain-compatible lesson design the expectation regardless of the best practice in use.

Identify the Passionate Champions

Passionate champions—a term coined by Phil Harkins in *Powerful Conversations: How High Impact Leaders Communicate* (1999)—are momentum-builders. These are individuals who are trusted within an organization to bring others along to accomplish the mission. In short, they embrace the philosophy that "impossible" just takes a little longer, never entertaining the idea of *not* reaching targeted goals.

Take, for example, Jen Morris, a middle school librarian and former English teacher who is a passionate champion for quality literacy instruction. Jen is also a staunch advocate for using brain-compatible strategies to help students learn. Her belief that middle school students should be readers and writers—and enjoy it in the process—generated a school-wide effort to model what *good* readers and writers do. In a time when many teachers are bemoaning the disinterest in reading and writing that befalls students in the middle grades, Jen Morris consistently leads a passionate conversation about literacy instruction resulting in her colleagues' high expectations and the positive responses of students.

Who are the passionate champions in your school? Is it you? Is there a literacy leader, administrator, or fellow teacher who can help you champion the cause of "teaching smarter" and organizing action groups or a study group to start learning about the brain trying new brain-compatible techniques?

Establish Instructional "Look-Fors"

As we saw in Chapter 5, look-fors are the criteria developed to inform students what is expected on a given project, task or test—they help students understand clearly what they must include and the level of performance that is expected. And when students help create the look-fors, they endorse or buy into the project.

Consider making an instructional look-for to guide your practice in a subject area. The look-for will outline what an observer should be able to pinpoint during any lesson you teach. Knowing exactly what is expected and where the proverbial bar has been set establishes targets for teachers to move toward. For example, the following survey was used as a guide by a committee of teachers and administrators asked to identify excellence in math instruction. These same indicators, compiled from the National Council of Teachers of Mathematics (NCTM) and other standards, can be used as math classroom look-fors at all levels, as shown in the example below. Look-for guidelines can be found in the Appendix on page 125.

Standards-Based Math Instruction Look-Fors

Indicator

LEARNING ENVIRONMENT

- ❐ The learning environment supports and encourages mathematical reasoning.
- ❐ The learning environment is nonthreatening and supports the participation of *all* students.
- ❐ Students are affirmed for asking questions and for innovative solutions.
- ❐ Students are encouraged to accept challenges and persist when errors occur.
- ❐ Mathematics instruction starts where the students are presently achieving based on pretesting.
- ❐ The teacher recognizes that students learn mathematics at different rates and in different ways.
- ❐ The students are provided with time for independent practice of concepts taught.

FOCUS ON UNDERSTANDING

- ❐ Students communicate their mathematical ideas in both oral and written forms.
- ❐ Students are encouraged to reread the problem and check responses.
- ❐ All mathematics students reflect on their own thinking and learning *(metacognition)* and document their understanding in math journals.
- ❐ There is an expectation that students will learn from the thinking of others as strategies are shared.
- ❐ The interrelatedness of mathematics topics with other content is established and applied (rather than presenting them it as a disjointed collection of topics).
- ❐ Proficiency of mastered concepts is systematically maintained by embedding review and recycling key concepts.

PROBLEM SOLVING

- ❐ Before assigning a task, the teacher anticipates student questions then models by solving the problem and demonstrating possible approaches through "think-aloud" strategies.

- ❐ Problem solving related to real-life situations across content areas is embedded into instruction.
- ❐ Students explore open-ended problems and extend the answers to those problems.
- ❐ Computation skills are taught through real-life problem solving.

ASSESSMENT

- ❐ A range of assessment procedures are used which reflect the approaches to teaching and learning mentioned above.
- ❐ The teacher provides regular assessment and feedback.
- ❐ The students assess their own work using scoring guides and/or other assessment tools.
- ❐ "Look-fors" and/or rubrics are provided to clarify expectations for students.

CONSTRUCTING FOR MEANING

- ❐ Classroom practice reflects the role of the teacher as a facilitator actively working to make sense of mathematics.
- ❐ The teacher takes on different roles: guide, coach, observer, facilitator, and model.
- ❐ The teacher's instruction reflects the understanding that learning mathematics requires "construction," not simply passive reception and rote recall.
- ❐ The teacher builds on prior knowledge of students to support mathematical concepts being taught.
- ❐ Effective questioning techniques encourage students to *think about* the concept being taught.
- ❐ Each student is actively involved in constructing meaning and applying knowledge to new learning.
- ❐ The teacher provides the students with access to a variety of manipulatives to build understanding and application.

STUDENT INVOLVEMENT

- ❐ The teacher recognizes the importance of using a variety of instructional formats (small groups, individual explorations, peer instruction, whole-class discussions, project work).
- ❐ Small-group instruction is utilized to differentiate based on student progress.
- ❐ Guidelines are set up for small-group work and conveyed to students.
- ❐ A variety of instructional strategies (nonverbal representation, graphic organizers, cooperative learning, etc.) are used to enhance instruction.
- ❐ Individual explorations and project work are encouraged.
- ❐ Rubrics are established identifying criteria for group work, projects, and individual explorations.

TECHNOLOGY USE

- ❐ Students utilize computers when learning and doing mathematics.
- ❐ The teacher uses graphing calculator technology effectively.
- ❐ Students receive accurate instruction on graphing calculator procedures.
- ❐ Students use graphing calculator technology to solve equations.
- ❐ The focus of discussions and the tone of the classroom are aimed at understanding mathematics, rather than simply going through computation steps on the calculator.

Make a Stop-Doing List

Teaching smarter can't be done by adding brain-compatible instruction on top of what exists already; rather, it displaces old practice. Although focusing on what *not* to do may seem negative, if you want to have renewal in the classroom, it is appropriate to declare that some things just shouldn't be done!

Jim Collins, author of *Good to Great* (2001), asserts that a stop-doing list is as important, if not more so, than a to-do list. He explains that great companies are intentional about the stop-doing list and discontinue—or unplug—practices that are extraneous or don't lead to the desired results. In classrooms, schools, and school systems—and at state and federal government levels, as well—debates exist about what to do and what to stop doing. I exercise my voice at these levels and encourage each of you to do so; regardless, the first level of impact is your classroom. So . . . what is your personal stop-doing list? Here are three of mine:

- **Never say the lesson has been taught unless all students have learned.** I constantly remind myself that the first step to taking ownership of the achievement of every student in a class is believing that "I haven't taught until all my students have learned!" I take into account the students who will succeed regardless of my efforts, the ones who need coaching and some prodding, and the ones who need serious, deep instruction and support. The content isn't the be-all and end-all—the student is!

- **Discard the mind-set that teacher-directed instruction is the most efficient way to keep up with the pacing.** I resist the urge to lecture students by reminding myself that lecturing is *not* the best way to get information into students' long-term memories. Teacher talk may cover the content—but because the students aren't doing the work, most don't absorb it. Instead, I focus on creating opportunities for students to direct their own learning through social interactions and a variety of strategies that keep them active and involved, such as those described in Chapter 6. If teacher talk is over 50 to 60 percent of the class, then students are not doing enough of the work!

- **Eliminate the notion that you can create a powerful lesson for the next day, ten minutes after school with a few notes in the margin of a planning book.** I avoid planning in a rush to get to another task. Instead, I use a structure for lesson design that ensures I am intentional about all that I do—and the students are much more involved, which sets the stage for students' growth and achievement.

When dedicated teachers reflect openly and honestly on best practices in the classroom, they have no trouble creating a stop-doing list. I challenge you to work with your grade-level and department colleagues to consider what procedures and practices are in place that are inconsistent with brain-compatible teaching.

I Taught It . . . I Think?

Years ago, a popular comic strip illustrated a boy with his dog in tow saying to another child, "I taught Stripe how to whistle!" The skeptical child responded, "I don't hear him whistling." The boy retorted, "Hey, I said I taught him how to whistle—I didn't say he learned it!" As a teacher, I raised an eyebrow when I read what was intended to be a humorous commentary and considered the not-so-subtle message. How often do we forge ahead in our pacing guides, assess and dispense grades, and tell ourselves "I taught it; I can't help it if they didn't learn it"?

Acknowledge Colleagues Who Are on Board

Years ago, I decided to get a pilot's license. I remember my flight instructor telling me that when a pilot informs the control tower about the need for an emergency landing, the air traffic controller queries back, "How many souls on board?" I encourage teachers to ask the same question as we move forward with the critical initiative to transform schools into institutions of teaching smarter. We don't need bodies—we need souls—and identifying the souls on board is an important part of the process.

Many of the souls supporting instructional initiatives are passionate champions in their own right—the cheerleaders, the models, the advocates for necessary changes. Others are teachers who have observed excellent practitioners work with students and have taken notice of ways to adjust their own instruction for greater impact. These dedicated teachers soon begin to mirror the methods they have observed and with mentoring and additional modeling begin to internalize best practice. Thus, an each one, reach one effect begins to occur as teachers—and administrators—help one another develop professionally.

Stick to the Message

A significant challenge in schools today is to hold steady and not let adverse winds steer you off course. Some of these winds seem overwhelming—school board members who have agendas, hot-off-the-press programs, a new and better way to teach to the test, a fresh regime of administrators who did it another way somewhere else, resistant colleagues, and so on. Sticking to the message may sometimes require you to be a broken record declaring the mission, over and over and over again: In this school, we expect teachers to be familiar *with and practice brain-compatible lesson design—and we all use these specific guidelines. We expect students to do the work of thinking and teachers to guide learning—and here is how we do it. We believe that students should be engaged at all times—and our instructional coach will be glad to model for best-practice teaching.*

Sticking to the message also means that whenever a hot new idea or method comes knocking at the door, the school staff—both teachers and administrators—use their filters to question whether or not the prospective program is consistent with "how we do things." For example, with the national emphasis on test taking and step-by-step pacing guides, there has been a boom in services that offer to help improve test results. If the mission of your classroom, school, or school division is to teach for deep understanding (and I hope it is) and these programs promote sit-at-the-desk, daily test-taking practice where the answer is the be-all and end-all and the conceptual understandings are secondary—then don't do it. Be discriminating about what you add to your plate; at the same time, be resolved about sticking to the message.

The bottom line, is the greatest difference in learning is made at the closest point of delivery—and that is the classroom teacher. Thus, the make or break of sticking to the message is the individual teacher—you. I know teachers who apply the brain-compatible principles against great odds, but they believe it and do it. Powerful teaching—even if done against the tide—is still powerful.

Involve Students

I am always amazed and rewarded when I have the opportunity to ask students what they think about school. Interest surveys, climate surveys, student-created look-fors, and self-assessments are all ways to get input and students at all levels welcome the chance to share their ideas. Similar to my questioning of the seniors mentioned earlier who described how they learned best, I asked a related question to a group of fifth graders "What is unfair about school?" The following responses are among those I received:

- Teachers telling me I did something when I didn't
- Teachers not letting me do the games and fun activities, because I don't finish my work in time
- The principal making us walk in a line back from lunch
- The PE teacher making us run around the field twice
- Being kept from recess because I forgot my homework
- Letting some students get away with talking . . . when I don't

- Waiting for other students to finish when I'm done

- Not being able to read books when I want to

Many insights can be gained when students are given a voice with an open-ended question. If we never ask for their opinions or ideas, how will *we* learn? When I received the input above, I shared the information with teachers and asked them to think about the messages we might learn from these fifth graders—messages about teaching styles, learning styles, differentiation, classroom management, and more. When students believe teachers really listen and care about what they think, the results are stronger connections and more investment in what is going on in the classroom and school.

Provide Opportunities for Meaningful Participation

"Adopting an attitude that views students as resources rather than as passive objects or problems is the critical foundation for this step. Never do in schools what students can do should become a motto, and each aspect of school should be analyzed for opportunities to give students more participation" (Henderson and Milstein, 2003, p. 29).

Audit Your Practice

Are we really doing what we say we're doing? The only way to be sure that the hoped-for best practice is being implemented in the classroom is to have criteria that outline expectations and colleagues to confirm through observation. Auditing practice is not the same as evaluating teachers, though they overlap. Ideally, auditing practice should be a natural result of teachers in learning communities making a request such as "I have been working with strategies to involve students in higher-level thinking. Would one of you have thirty minutes during your planning time to observe my class this week?" An administrator might plan to facilitate audits in this way: "We introduced the literacy program two years ago and have provided materials, training, and criteria. Let's set up teams of teachers to visit classroom in schools other than their own to observe if instruction is aligned with the look-fors."

In a way, a program audit is action research where observers search for evidence that targeted goals are being met. I see it as somewhat akin to the weight-loss programs. As uncomfortable as it may be, the weekly weigh-in helps to hold the participants' feet to the fire. If auditing programs were a matter of course—supported by teachers and administrators alike as a meaningful way to make sure we are doing what we say we're doing, then teachers would demonstrate mastery more quickly. The lesson design checklist on page 124 is a strong basis for auditing instruction.

As you collaborate with your colleagues to gain new insights on learning and the brain and apply these understandings daily in the classroom, you will become the inspiration to those who follow. Teaching smarter using research on the brain and learning transforms instruction by engaging the minds and, yes, souls of students. May you go forward with unwaivering commitment and enjoy the journey!

Reflection

1. Select a key standard that you will be teaching and an assignment related to it that you will ask students to complete. Develop a list of six to ten criteria (look-fors) for that help define your expectations and that you can share with students.

2. Select three things related to teaching that you think should be on your stop-doing list. Share this information with a colleague or your team members to see if there are items in common.

3. Who are the passionate champions in your school and school system? How can the school leaders help these individuals and all teachers thrive on the journey to teaching smarter?

4. Review the criteria for "Brain-Compatible Lesson Design." Agree on two focus areas that will help you teach smarter. Outline the first four to five steps you plan to take to get started.

References

Anderson, L. W., & Krathwold, D. R. (2000). *A taxonomy for learning, teaching, and assessing: A revision of Bloom's taxonomy of educational objectives*. Boston: Allyn & Bacon.

Blakemore, S., & Frith, U. (2005). *The learning brain: Lessons for education*. Malden, MA: Blackwell Publishing Company.

Blakeslee, S. (2006, January 10). Cells that read minds. *The New York Times*.

Bloom, B. S. (1976). *Human characteristics and school learning*. New York: John Wiley.

Brown, A. L. (1988). Motivation to learn and understand: On taking charge of one's own learning. *Cognition and instruction, 5*(4), 311–321.

Collins, J. (2001). *Good to great: Why some companies make the leap... and others don't*. New York: HarperCollins.

Csibra, G. (2005) Mirror neurons and action observation: Is simulation involved? *Interdisciplines*. Retrieved September 23, 2007 from http://www.interdisciplines.org/mirror/papers/4

Darling-Hammond, L. (1997). *The right to learn*. San Francisco: Jossey-Bass.

Danielson, C., & McGreal, T. L. (2000). *Teacher evaluation to enhance professional practice*. Princeton, NJ: Educational Testing Service. Retrieved October 6, 2007 from http://www.chss.iup.edu/jrmcdono/ED455-methods/teacher_evaluation_to_enhance_pr.htm

Davis, D. (2000). *Writing as a second language: From experience to story to prose*. Little Rock, AK: August House.

Dufour, R., Eaker, R., & Dufour, R. (2005). *On common ground: The power of professional learning communities*. Bloomington, IN: National Education Service.

Elias, M. J., Zins, J. E., Weissberg, R. P., Frey, K. S., Greenberg, M. T., Norris, M. H., et al. (1997). *Promoting social and emotional learning: Guidelines for educators*. Alexandria, VA: Association for Supervision and Curriculum Development.

Etnier, J. L., Salazar, W., Landers, D. M., Petruzzello, S. J., Han, M., & Nowell, P. (1997). The influence of physical fitness and exercise upon cognitive functioning: A meta-analysis. *Journal of Sport & Exercise Psychology, 19*(3), 249–277.

Evers, S., & Suhr, B. (2000). Changes of the neurotransmitter serotonin but not of hormones during short time music perception. *European Archives of Psychiatry and Clinical Neuroscience, 250*(3), 144–147. Steinkopff. Retrieved August, 21, 2007 from http://www.springerlink.com/content/1nwl46m2pxe674ar/fulltext.pdf.

Foster, E., & Rotoloni, R. (2005). Reciprocal Teaching: General overview of theories. In M. Orey (Ed.), *Emerging perspectives on learning, teaching, and technology*. Retrieved August 2007 from http://projects.coe.uga.edu/epltt

Galewitz, H. (Ed.). (2001). *Music: a book of quotations*. Mineola, NY: Dover.

Goleman, D. (1996). *Emotional intelligence: Why it can matter more than I.Q.* New York: Bantam Books.

Gordon, W. J. (1961). *Synectics: The development of creative capacity*. New York: Harper and Row.

Harkins, P. (1999). *Powerful conversations: How high impact leaders communicate*. New York: McGraw-Hill.

Hashey, J. M., & Connors, D. J. (2003). Learn from our journey: Reciprocal teaching action research. *The Reading Teacher, 57*(3), 224–232.

Henderson, N., & Milstein, M. M. (2003). *Resiliency in schools*. Thousand Oaks, CA: Corwin Press.

Hyerle, D. (1996). *Visual tools for constructing knowledge*. Alexandria, VA: Association for Supervision and Curriculum Development.

Iacoboni, M. (2005). Understanding others: Imitation, language, empathy. In S. Hurley, & N. Chater (Eds.), *Perspectives on imitation: From mirror neurons to memes*. (Volume 1, Chapter 2.) Cambridge, MA: MIT Press.

Intrato, S. M. (2004). The engaged classroom. *Educational Leadership, 62*(1), 20–24.

Jacobs, H. H. (Consultant). (1992). Integrating the curriculum. *The Video Journal of Education, 2*(8) [Videotape]. Salt Lake City, UT: National Center for Outcomes Based Education.

Jehlen, A. (2001, January). Interview with Laurie Shepard: How to fight a "Death Star." *NEA Today*, Online Edition. Retrieved September 23, 2007, from http://findarticles.com/p/articles/mi_qa3617/is_n8953068/print

Jensen, E. (1995). *The learning brain*. Delmar, CA: Turning Point.

Jensen, E., & Dabney, M. (2000). *Learning smarter: The new science of teaching*. San Diego, CA: The Brain Store.

Jhamandas, A. (2002). How biological is music? *La scena musicale, 8*(2). Retrieved October 6, 2007, from http://www.scena.org/lsm/sm8-2/musique_biologie_en.htm

Johnson, D. W., Johnson, R. T., & Holubec, E. J. (1994). *Cooperative learning in the classroom*. Alexandria, VA: Association for Supervision and Curriculum Development.

Kagan, S. (1994). *Cooperative learning*. San Clemente, CA: Kagan Cooperative Learning.

Kovalik, S., & Olsen, K. (1997). *Integrated thematic instruction: The model* (3rd Ed.). Kent, WA: Susan Kovalik & Associates.

Kosslyn, S. M., Ganis, G., & Thompson, W. L. (2001). Neural foundations of imagery. *Nature Reviews: Neuroscience, 2*, 635–642. Retrieved September 16, 2007, from http://www.nature.com/reviews/neuro

Laubach Literacy Ontario. *Laubach chronology*. Retrieved September 22, 2007, from http://www.laubach-on.ca/laubachchronology.htm

Levitan, D. (2006). *This is your brain on music: The science of a human obsession*. New York: Plume.

Macon J. M., Bewell, D., & Vogt, M. E. (1991). *Responses to literature*. Newark, DE: International Reading Association.

Marzano, R. J., Pickering, D. J., & Pollock, J. E. (2001). *Classroom instruction that works*. Alexandria, VA: Association for Supervision and Curriculum Development.

McGaugh, J. L. (2003). *Memory and emotion: the making of lasting memories*. New York: Columbia University Press.

Mulligan, D. (2007, September). Improving SOL test results in all core subjects. Presentation at the annual meeting of the Virginia Association of School Superintendents, Roanoke, VA.

Palincsar, A. S., & Brown, A. L. (1984). Reciprocal teaching of comprehension-fostering and comprehension-monitoring activities. *Cognition and Instruction, 2*, 117–175.

Palincsar, A. S., & Brown, A. L. (1986). Interactive teaching to promote independent learning from text. *The Reading Teacher, 39*(8), 771–777.

Palincsar, A. S., & Klenk, L. (1991). *Learning dialogues to promoting text comprehension*. (PHS Grant 059). Bethesda, MD: National Institute of Health and Human Development.

Pascual-Leone, A., & Baillargeon, R. (1994). Developmental measurement of mental attention. *International Journal of Behavioral Development, 17*, 161–200.

Paul, R., & Elder, L. (2007). *The miniature guide to critical thinking: Concepts and tools*. The Foundation for Critical Thinking. Retrieved September 23, 2007, from www.criticalthinking.org

Pearson, P. D., Roehler, L. R., Dole, J. A., & Duffy, G. G. (1992). Developing expertise in reading comprehension. In S. J. Samuels & A. Farstrup (Eds.), *What research has to say about reading Instruction*, (2nd Ed.). Newark, DE: International Reading Association.

Ramachandran, V.S. (2000, June). Mirror neurons and imitation learning as the driving force behind "the great leap forward" in human evolution. *Edge*. Retrieved September 23, 2007, from http://www.edge.org/3rd_culture/ramachandran/ramachandran_p1.htm

Raphael, T. (1986). Teacher question-answer relationships, revised. *The Reading Teacher, 36*, 186–190.

Ratey, J. J. (2001). *A user's guide to the brain: Perception, attention, and the four theaters of the brain*. New York: Pantheon Books.

Ratey, J. J. (2008). *Spark: the revolutionary new science of exercise and the brain* (with E. Hagerman). New York: Little, Brown.

Renzulli, J. S. (Ed.). (1986). *Systems and models for developing programs for the gifted and talented*. Mansfield Center, CT: Creative Learning Press.

Resnick, L. B. (1999, June 16). Making America smarter. *Education Week Century Series, 18*(40), 38–40. Retrieved from http://www.edweek.org/ew/vol-18/40resnick.h18

Rizzolatti, G., & Craighero, L. (2005). Mirror neurons: A neurological approach to empathy. In J.P. Changeux, A. Damasio, W. Singer, & Y. Christen (Eds.), *Neurobiology of Human Values*, 107–123. Berlin: Springer-Verlag. Retrieved September 23, 2007, from http://www.liralab.it/projects/mirror

Robb, L. (2000) *Teaching reading in middle school*. New York: Scholastic.

Ruch, J. (2001). *The effects of fitness levels on cognitive processes*. Retrieved October 17, 2007 from http://www.hope.edu/academic/psychology/335/webrep2/fitness.htm

Shaywitz, S. (2005). *Overcoming dyslexia: A new and complete science-based program for reading problems at any level*. New York: Vintage Books.

Slavin, R. E. (1995) *Cooperative learning: Theory, research, and practice*, (2nd Ed.). Boston: Allyn & Bacon,

Sprenger, M. (1999). *Learning and memory: The brain in action*. Alexandria, VA: Association for Supervision and Curriculum Development.

Smith, A. (2005). *The brain's behind it: New knowledge about the brain and learning*. Norwalk, CT: Crown House.

Sousa, D. (2001). *How the brain learns*. Thousand Oaks, CA: Corwin Press.

Sylwester, R. (2005). *How to explain a brain: An educator's handbook of brain terms and cognitive processes*. Thousand Oaks, CA: Corwin Press.

Sylwester, R. (2006, December). Cognitive neuroscience: Discoveries and educational practices. *The School Administrator, 11*(63), *32–37.*

Taylor, R. *Divergent questioning models*. Curriculum Design for Excellence. Retrieved September 23, 2007, from http://www.rogertaylor.com

Torrance, P. (1984). The role of creativity in identification of the gifted and talented. *Gifted Child Quarterly, 28*, 153–156.

Valeo, T. (2007, March–April). Imaging sheds light on brain's wiring. *Brain Work: The Neuroscience Newsletter, 17*(2).

Wiggins, G., & McTighe, J. (1998). *Understanding by design*. Alexandria, VA: Association for Supervision and Curriculum Development.

Winerman, L. (2005, October). The mind's mirror. *Monitor on psychology, 36*(9). Retrieved September 23, 2007, from http://www.apa.org/monitor/oct05/mirror.html

Wolfe, P. (2001). *Brain matters: Translating research into classroom practice*. Alexandria, VA: Association for Supervision and Curriculum Development.

van Garderen, D. (2004). Reciprocal teaching as a comprehension strategy for understanding mathematical word problems. *Reading and Writing Quarterly, 20*(2), 225–229.

Virginia Department of Education. (2001). *Virginia standards of learning, civics and economics, (grade 7)*. Retrieved September 30, 2007 from http://www.pen.k12.va.us/VDOE/Superintendent/Sols/history7.pdf

Materials Cited

Arcangelos Chamber Ensemble. (1998). *Music for productivity* [CD]. The Center for Psychoacoustic Research. Ogden, UT: Advanced Brain Technologies.

Baylor, B. (1972). *When clay sings*. New York: Charles Scribner's Sons.

Baylor, B. (1975). *The desert is theirs*. New York: Charles Scribner's Sons.

Character Counts! (2007). Character Counts! National Office / Josephson Institute of Ethics, 9841 Airport Blvd., #300, Los Angeles, CA 90045. Retrieved September 20, 2007, from http://www.charactercounts.org

Drop Everything and Read (DEAR), K–12 teaching and learning, University of North Carolina at Chapel Hill, http://www.learnnc.org/glossary/Drop + Everything + and + Read

History Alive! Palo Alto, CA: Teacher's Curriculum Institute. Retrieved October 6, 2007, from http://www.teachtci.com

Integrating the Curriculum with Heidi Hayes Jacobs. (1992). [Videotape]. School Improvement Network, 8686 South 1300 East Sandy, UT 84094 and online at https://www.schoolimprovement.com/store/ index.cfm?action = ViewDetails&ItemID = 151&Category = 2

Lesson Design Reminders

❏ Is your classroom a respectful, nurturing classroom for students?

❏ Do you identify essential understandings of the lesson and "teach to the bullet"?

❏ Are you modeling what you want students to do using look-fors, rubrics, and/or a range of examples that they can study and critique?

❏ Do you activate students' prior knowledge before teaching new concepts?

❏ Do you establish the relevance of a topic and build connections based on students' own experiences?

❏ Do you teach to the task, planning with the key action verbs given in the learning standards and in the levels of Bloom's Taxonomy to guide you?

❏ Do you activate higher-level thinking during question/answer time and in assignments?

❏ Are you practicing the age-plus/minus-two-minutes rule to hold students' attention?

❏ Do you vary the activities and keep your students engaged throughout the lesson?

❏ Do you design lessons to build in less teacher talk and more student interaction?

❏ Do you provide students with hands-on activities?

❏ Do you involve students in cooperative group and partner learning experiences?

❏ Do you increase retention and memory by using:

- novelty in your teaching (i.e., props, costumes, unusual activities)? cognitive dissonance (i.e. asserting a controversial perspective)?

- non-linguistic representations (i.e., images, pictures to enhance note-taking, vocabulary)?

- music to enhance the learning environment? To introduce concepts?

- songs, rhythms, rap to increase retention of content?

❏ Do you keep the primacy/recency rule in mind and ensure that:

- the first part of class is focused with clear statements about the lesson's learning goals?

- closure occurs at the end of the lesson highlighting the key points learned?

- exit tickets or other brief assessments are used for students to restate the key points of the lesson?

❏ Do you reteach for mastery, rather than "go over" to get the right answer?

Appendix

Guidelines for Creating Look-Fors

? Why Look Fors? Students perform at their highest levels when they are very clear about the expectations teachers have for them. Look-fors, or criteria lists, for class work and projects guide students and serve as tools of self-reflection, eliminating uncertainty.

? How Often? Teachers often ask, "Do I have to develop look-fors for every assignment?" No. If a math teacher asks students to do the odd questions at the end of a chapter, look-fors are not necessary. If the teacher asks students to complete an illustrated poster of the real-life uses of three kinds of triangles, look-fors are needed. The frequency with which you use them will depend on the products or performances you ask students to deliver in your daily plans.

? When are look-fors essential? Develop look-fors any time the assignment has two or more components, such as research and presentation. Look-fors are also needed also when you want to assess a range of skills such as organization, illustrations, format, and neatness. In addition, use look-fors when the task is cumulative and you need to outline specific elements that you want students to include.

? Are look-fors just for students? No. Clear expectations are important for teachers as well and can support you in your professional growth. You might use look-fors to help you set up a Writer's Workshop, self-evaluate your performance teaching a particular subject area (see the mathematics instruction look-for on page 114), or use brain-compatible instruction in your lesson design (see the checklist on page 124).

? Is there a standard format? Look-fors typically list the criteria on the left and a recording system on the right. The criteria can be in statement or question format and can be as short as two or three bullets or as long as is appropriate. (See the examples below.)

Look-Fors: Poster Project
(upper-elementary/middle school)

	Possible Points	Earned Points
The topic/theme of the poster is clear to the viewer.	10	
There are 5 to 7 supportive ideas for the theme.	20	
The information on the poster is accurate and shows thorough understanding of the topic.	30	
Illustrations and pictures support the topic and add to the effectiveness of the poster	15	
Space, textures and color enhance both the content and look of the poster.	10	
The poster is appealing as a whole and does not seem like a collection of information.	15	

Look-For: Differentiated Instruction
(professional development)

	Always	Sometimes	Seldom	Never
I differentiate using assessment data using				
A. interest surveys				
C. brain-compatible indicators				
D. student self assessment reflections				
E. pre- and post-test results				
I differentiate the content level of the material using				
A. different levels of textbooks				
B. leveled resource materials				
D. manipulatives				

Building a Thinking Classroom

Indicate the degree to which you think your students meet the criteria below.
(5 = Highest; 1 = Lowest)

When you incorporate thinking skills into your teaching, you want to know whether students are increasing their ability to think critically and creatively. One way to evaluate students' thinking is to observe how often they exhibit certain key behaviors. Please rate these positive-thinking behaviors.

Perseverance—Do your students...

1. Stick with it when trying to solve problems, answer questions and complete assignments?	5	4	3	2	1
2. Work the problem from a different angle if they don't succeed?	5	4	3	2	1
3. Analyze problems following a logical sequence of steps?	5	4	3	2	1

Use of prior knowledge—Do your students...

4. Make connections between what they already know and a new concept?	5	4	3	2	1
5. Use prior knowledge to assist in the learning task? (Students say, "This topic reminds me of..." or, "This is like the time we...")	5	4	3	2	1

Metacognition—Are your students able to...

6. Tell you the thinking that led them to their answers?	5	4	3	2	1
7. List the steps involved in completing a task and describe where they are in that sequence?	5	4	3	2	1
8. Indicate at what point they ran into difficulty?	5	4	3	2	1
9. Describe their thinking at the point of difficulty?	5	4	3	2	1
10. "Think aloud" as to why a choice was made or response given.	5	4	3	2	1
11. Describe the steps they took to complete the task successfully?	5	4	3	2	1
12. Support their responses by referring back to the text?	5	4	3	2	1
13. Articulate an issue or problem from numerous perspectives?	5	4	3	2	1
14. Clearly explain how they arrived at an interpretation or conclusion?	5	4	3	2	1

Reflectiveness—Do your students...

15. Think before answering?	5	4	3	2	1
16. Take time to understand instructions before beginning a task?	5	4	3	2	1
17. Plan their steps so erasures are kept to a minimum?	5	4	3	2	1

Problem solving—Do your students...

18. Ask questions and identify problems on their own?	5	4	3	2	1
19. Ask their peers questions like, "How do you know that's true?" or, "What do you think that?"	5	4	3	2	1
20. Search for and use information that is clear, accurate, and relevant?	5	4	3	2	1

Flexibility—Are your students...

21. Comfortable with ambiguity? (answers don't come right away)	5	4	3	2	1
22. Willing to consider alternative points of view?	5	4	3	2	1
23. Able to evaluate the consequence of different actions?	5	4	3	2	1

Precise language—Do your students...

24. Use quality descriptive words and analogies to describe objects, people, and ideas?	5	4	3	2	1
25. Avoid use of slang and vague terms such as *cool*, *good*, *okay*.	5	4	3	2	1

Enjoyment of thinking—Do your students...

26. Welcome situations which require them to think?	5	4	3	2	1
27. Exhibit an "I can" attitude when confronted with thinking tasks?	5	4	3	2	1
28. Find answers on their own, without help from you?	5	4	3	2	1

Transference

29. Students use their thinking skills both in and out of class.	5	4	3	2	1
30. Other teachers say your students use high-level thinking strategies.	5	4	3	2	1

Index